THE
MOMPOWERMENT
GUIDE TO
WORK-LIFE BALANCE

The Mompowerment Guide to Work-Life Balance:

Insights from Working Moms on Balancing Career and Family

SUZANNE BROWN

KAT BIGGIE PRESS
Columbia, SC

Published by Kat Biggie Press.
Columbia, SC 29229
http://katbiggiepress.com

Cover design by The Higgins Creative and Robert Paulsen
Book design Write.Publish.Sell
Edited by Betsy Rhame-Minor

ISBN-13: 978-1-948604-12-3
Library of Congress Control Number: 2018953746
First Edition: September 2018

10 9 8 7 6 5 4 3 2 1

CONTENTS

PART V:
The Personal Side of Work-Life Balance

DEDICATION

To my husband, Robert, thank you for your support and love. And to my boys, A and E, thank you for your love and enthusiasm.

A NOTE TO THE READER

THE FIRST *MOMPOWERMENT* BOOK and subsequent research focused on professional part-time working moms. What I realized as I looked at trends and advice from the more than 110 interviews that I did for that book was that most working moms could use the tips, tricks, insights, and advice garnered from the interviews and my experience and research, regardless of industry, level, or career approach.

One by one, the women I interviewed opened up their lives, answering my questions, sharing lessons they learned and successes they've had, so other moms can benefit. Their stories were full of information on all aspects of their lives.

And, on this amazing journey, I have personally learned so much from these stories and all the advice, insights, and challenges. These moms have pushed me to think differently about my own approach to work-life balance.

Our younger son was born and our older son was in the advanced stages of active toddlerhood (our pediatrician calls this stage "the tantrum threes") while I was doing the research for the first book. I was thrilled to have such a wealth of information on creating more balance from moms who knew. I quickly integrated tips and advice into my own life time and time again from the moms who shared their stories.

I know that when you look for advice on your career as a working mom, there is plenty out there. And much of it is designed to help you be that much more amazing and successful in your career. I set out to write a different kind of book. I wanted to be more informative and practical in how I help working moms think about their work-life balance. I share tips, hacks, advice, and insights, some of which you can implement tomorrow. I want to help working moms think differently about work-life balance, so that they feel empowered in their careers, in their lives at home, and in balancing the two.

And, for that matter, we're really talking about balancing all the things and that is more than work versus life. For the purpose of this book, we'll call it work-life balance since that is the term most often used. After all we're trying to balance work, which a huge part of the day, with all the other things. Whether you call it work-life balance, balancing all the things, or simply balance, as working moms we need more of it in our lives.

And, while I could write about work-life balance for all professionals, the lens I use to write this book is that of a mom. It's what I know and who I see in the mirror each day. It also reflects who I spoke with in the interviews for this book.

Maybe you're about to have your first child. While there are books on how to make the most of maternity leave and on how to be amazing once you return from maternity leave to your same job, what about the moms who realize they might want to think differently about work when they get back? That is one way to look at the information in this book.

You might be reading or even rereading this book with the birth of your second child, when juggling a career and home life becomes that much more complex. And you may read the advice and suggestions differently when you're juggling more things.

Perhaps you're reading this book as you start to think about having a family. It could be helpful to think through the aspects I mention about industry and what companies offer, even before you choose a company to work for, even before becoming a mom for the first time.

This is especially important if you'd like to stay in an industry or at a company long-term.

The idea is to get tips and insights in these pages that you can use outright, or you might find ideas that trigger other ideas and solutions for your situation. Take what makes sense and leave behind what doesn't (or maybe it doesn't for now). And adjust whatever tips, hacks, or advice you see here to make them work for you.

You will see that each chapter has a summary at the end. If there is a chapter with information that you feel very confident about and you might want to skip it, take a look at the summary to see if there is anything you still might want to check out in that specific chapter.

My hope is that in these pages, you find ways to overcome the challenges that you face. I want to help you create a situation where you feel empowered in career and motherhood and the balance between.

You won't have to figure things out alone. I'm here with you on your journey. I'll help you uncover how you can have the life you want that combines career and family the way you want.

To help in your own situation, in addition to the ideas and exercises throughout the book, you can find templates and worksheets to download at **www.mompowerment.com/booktemplates**.

My biggest hope is that you find this information useful and that it helps you on your path to figuring out what works for you and your family. Enjoy!

PART I

AN INTRODUCTION TO WORK-LIFE BALANCE FOR WORKING MOMS

CHAPTER 1
YOU ARE NOT ALONE

All the Stories

You're a full-time working mom who loves her career, but you're finding you need a bit more balance. You're not alone if you feel that you could be better at work-life balance. A study showed that 60 percent of working moms find work-life balance difficult.[1]

Is it that you feel you need to be more efficient with your time? How can you be better about completing what you *must* do so you have more time to do the things you *want to* do?

Is it that you feel like you're missing out on important moments in your child's life? Or maybe you're needing to take on more of the care of your aging parents?

You're realizing you need to spend more time focusing on your child. You weren't fully prepared when the pediatrician started talking about your son's speech delay. You thought something was a bit off, but this is another level. Your mother has offered to take him to speech therapy, but you want to be the one to do it. How can you better utilize your time so that these extra three hours won't mean staying even later at the office. You feel like you're already at the office more than you'd like to be. And you don't want to step away from your career, so transitioning to a stay-at-home situation isn't even on the table.

Your daughter is now a preteen and is having a rough go, because that happens at this age. (Although challenging moments happen at any age, right?) You're finding yourself wanting to be around more, but how can that happen with everything you have going on at work? Could you figure out a way to be more available to your daughter and stay engaged at work? How can you make that happen?

You've noticed your parents are having more health issues as illnesses linger and they deal with more and more aches and pains. What will you do if they need more of your attention when you're already squeezed between your own family obligations and work? How can you fit more into your already busy day?

What happens when you get back from maternity leave? You love sitting and snuggling with your child. And that baby smell! And it's such a long day away! Is there a way to finish your work day earlier and get home to see your sweet baby without having to hop back on later?

You're trying to be the best mom, wife, employee, friend, sibling, daughter, and everything else that you can. It's getting harder and harder though. If only you could create more flexibility in the next few years to be more engaged with your family.

Do any of these sound like your own story? Each story is from a mom I interviewed or have since spoken with. These aren't unusual situations for moms though.

I get it. We all get it. Motherhood is rewarding, amazing, magical, and all things incredible. Let's face it, being a mom can also be hard. Being a working mom with a career, maybe even a demanding career, is even more challenging. You're not alone in feeling this pull to be engaged in your child's life and yet you don't want to walk away from your career.

Who Did I Interview?

I spoke with moms at various levels, although the women I spoke with tended to be more seasoned and have more experience. These moms have worked an average of fourteen to fifteen years. They work in a variety of industries, such as financial services, education, consulting, medicine, engineering, accounting, marketing, and beauty, to name a few.

They live across the United States although the vast majority live in larger cities or the surrounding suburbs (about 96 percent). The rest either have a work-from-home situation with their employer or work for themselves.

About 62 percent of the moms work for a company, in both large and small businesses. The other roughly 38 percent are entrepreneurs (or "mompreneurs," if you prefer) who started their own businesses.

They know their own strengths and understand what they bring to the table. They are often in leadership positions, though not always the team lead, and are decision-makers. They have figured out how to be more efficient and effective with their time, and you can learn from what they're doing that works for them to get ideas on what could work for you.

In summary:

There is no specific type of industry, location, or type of role in which working moms who spoke with me can be found.

- Working moms are in all sorts of industries and roles across the US.
- The advice in this book generally comes from seasoned career women with fourteen to fifteen years of experience.
- Some moms created a new business to find more work-life balance.

CHAPTER 2

WHY NOW?

You might be wondering why I decided to write this book now. It seems like we're at a turning point. Companies, leadership, and even government are finally talking about aspects of the workplace that impact working moms in the United States. Additionally, more and more conversations are happening about work-life balance and the positive impact it has on employees at the office and at home.

Maternity Leave and Then What?

At the time that this was written, the conversation was finally starting in companies and even at some levels of government on the topic of maternity leave. An increasing number of companies are starting to offer paid time off for moms to spend weeks or even months with their newborns to bond, establish rhythms, and allow their bodies to recuperate from giving birth. A recent study by the Society of Human Resource Management and Families at Work Institute polled 899 businesses across the United States. They found that, "Overall, 75 percent of employers with 50 or more employees provide 12 or more weeks of maternity leave."[1] About 58 percent of companies offer some level of paid maternity leave.[2]

What happens after those two, three, or even six months of maternity leave? Interestingly, this is in comparison to three to twelve months or more of paid leave in other developed countries.[3]

We're hearing more about maternity leave, but what about the early development years of childhood? Studies show the importance of this young age—years two through four—in a child's development. A Harvard study explains how the pathways that develop in the brain in these early years impact lifelong "learning, behavior, and health."[4] The emotional foundation is formed at this stage as well.[5] So much is happening at this moment in a child's development and some moms want to miss as little as possible. How can they though, if they're working full time, especially in demanding jobs that don't allow for a lot of time with family?

What about Moms of Older Kids?

How do moms stay or get involved in the lives of their older children who might have activities where they practice and compete after school and on weekends? What about moms simply being available to their kids, who need guidance during the preteen or teenage years? Several of the moms shared that their older children needed mom to be around even more, to go from one place to another or for encouragement during these sometimes tough years in a child's development.

If you have a typical approach to your day, you might not get to be that involved in your kids' activities. You'll provide support to your family at dinner, bedtime, or on the weekends. Maybe, though, using some ideas from this book can help you either make yourself more available during the day, if your children need to get a hold of you. Or maybe using ideas from this book will help you carve out time to participate more in all the goings-on of your older kids, whether attending, coaching, or simply getting kids from one place to another.

Moms are Getting Sandwiched

Caring for children is not the only challenge that moms are facing when it comes to taking care of their families. At the time that this book was written, consider that roughly 10,000 Baby Boomers turn retirement age every day, which will continue for at least a decade.[6] Who will care for this aging population? In many households, the duties of childcare *and* caring for parents/parents in-law fall to moms.

This is something that women are trying to change, but for now, those duties fall mainly on moms' shoulders. Moms are essentially getting sandwiched and their time is getting squeezed between caring for their children and their parents or in-laws, on top of trying to manage their careers. If this scenario sounds familiar, you're not alone. Start talking to other women at your employer to see who is being squeezed by care for family and care for aging relatives. Come together as a group to have an open, honest conversation with senior management about necessary changes to accommodate the challenge of caring for aging family members. If more moms talk about this type of challenge, the company will start looking at solutions for a large group, instead of many private conversations between moms and their managers about each situation.

Changes in Generations

I was curious about how different generations approach work-life balance. I am sharing a bit of that here, since that can help us see why now is a good time to focus more on work-life balance for working moms.

Generation X Moms in the Workplace

You don't find a lot of information on Generation X in the workplace. I admit that I was intrigued by the information on Generation X that I found. Gen X is my generation. I saw so much of my own perspective and underlying beliefs explained. And, since it's rare to find this information spelled out in easily accessible places, I thought it was helpful to include it here.

Gen X has come up with countless advances for women along the way. According to Hannah Ubl, a generation expert at Bridge-Works, a generational consulting company, "It was Gen X women who paved the way for work-life balance–maternity leave, nursing rooms at work, [and] flexible hours."[7]

Part of why Gen X women are different than their Millennial counterparts is that "Gen X women have more life challenges [going on],"[8] says Tacy M. Byham, PhD, CEO of Development Dimensions International, a global leadership consultancy. She shares that, "Millennial women may or may not have kids, but gen-Xers have kids and aging parents. Those life circumstances become a barometer for where they want to go and how fast."[9]

Simply based on age, experience, and education, Gen Xers are often in middle to senior management positions at work at this point. This might be precisely where you find yourself as you're contemplating a new position, which will result in a lot more hours at work and/or maybe you'll find yourself more stressed because of more responsibility. And that's not necessarily what you're looking for at this point of your life.

Ubl shares that there is the idea that "it is often their strong commitment to family that prevents them from going after a promotion, because they feel they need to take care of their kids or their elderly parents first."[10] Where does this need come from? What makes these moms maybe even take a break from their careers as they focus on family, whether their own children or parents?

In large part, the answers seem to be from the environment that Gen Xers grew up in. Think back to your childhood. Maybe you were a "latchkey kid," one of the countless kids who had a key around your neck to let you into your house because *both* parents were working. Gen X was the first generation where this was common.[11]

According to BridgeWorks, "Many Xers were left to fend for themselves after school. As many as 40% of Gen Xers were latchkey kids. . . . They learned to be independent early on . . . getting their homework done . . . and no one was hovering over them. . . ."[12]

And today, we still don't need that push from our managers and senior leaders. We make things happen in any environment, including work-from-home or in flexible schedule arrangements, because that's what we do. With that in mind, we expect our managers and senior leadership to trust us to get things done without being under their watchful eye.

Gen X moms are also specifically looking for work-life balance. They "reject the notion that more hours in the office [equals] a more productive, hard-working employee."[13] They will be incredibly productive to do whatever it takes to get to their child's activities and to focus on family after work hours.[14]

Having it All

Gen X women were constantly exposed to "the women's movement," where women could have it all.[15] I remember the constant examples, even in commercials on television (in the days before people skipped ads). I'm not alone in thinking I was sold a bag of goods about having it all. I can't count the number of women I've spoken to who work full time and have said that it's not really possible to have it all. And I will say, that based on the common version of having it all, that's true.

And that's the key to Gen X. We want this focus on family and we want to succeed at work. We're willing to change what "success" means so that we have it all.

Considering all the things that Gen X has already done for women, we're clearly willing to make advances for other women as we go. We're working on redefining what being a working mom looks like for ourselves and the women moving up the ranks behind us.

Gen Xers and Entrepreneurship

I've talked about women in the workplace largely as it relates to women at employers. What's interesting is that many Gen Xers are entrepreneurs. When you think of a start-up, you might have the image of a bunch of twenty-somethings with a new, brilliant idea often related to technology. Most people I've spoken with think of young people when you say start-up. According to a 2015 study by The Sage Group, a software provider for small and medium businesses, about 55 percent of start-ups are Generation Xers. That same study shows that 57 percent of start-ups are founded by women, largely for more work-life balance.[16]

According to Bridgepoint, "[Generation X is] leading the workforce as innovative . . . contributors, and are at the forefront of some of the most disruptive workplace shifts we've seen to date."[17] Generation X has been bringing innovation into the workplace for some time. It's how we think. This ability to think outside of the box (because, really, who has time for staying in a box) is what makes Gen X moms an integral group to bring a new way of working to companies and as entrepreneurs. With Gen Xers driving so much change already, sometimes below the radar with their head down and get-it-done mentality, it makes sense that Gen X will help drive the change necessary to make work-life balance more commonplace in businesses, big and small.

Millennials

Millennials create another layer of the work-life balance conversation. It turns out that part of what sets Millennials apart from previous generations, as it relates to this book, is that they start their careers looking for work-life balance, and not necessarily because of family obligations. In the Millennials at Work/Reshaping the Workplace survey done by the consulting firm PwC, 95 percent of Millennial respondents described work-life balance as important and 70 percent said it was *very* important. [18]

Millennials are interested in work-life integration, blending work and life together instead of trying to balance the two separately.[19] And a driver behind that is flexibility and using technology to enable all of these things to come together.[20] For example, they want to work several hours and then leave the office to go workout, spend time with friends, participate in a hobby activity, or learn something new, and come back to work afterward.[21]

Millennial Mom Interviews

I spoke with several moms from the Millennial generation. And their stories, especially for the moms who are entrepreneurs, were different from those of the Generation X moms in their approach to motherhood and combining career and family.

One Millennial mom in the Boston area shared that she worked for several years and then resigned, so that she and her fiancée could travel around South America for five months. And when she came back, she didn't go back into the workforce. She started her own Etsy shop making jewelry so that she had flexibility for her future family instead of working really hard for a few more years and then pulling back once having kids.

A Millennial mom, who owns a children's clothing boutique and entertainment venue in Brentwood, California, shared, "my family is embedded into the store" and "entangled in my business." She describes the two as "intertwined."

Another mom who does creative design and branding near Denver, Colorado, explains that life isn't quite so divided. She describes it as a "messy blend of work and family." That approach works for her and many from her generation who I've spoken to since.

Millennials in the Workplace

Millennials' influence on the workplace is just getting started. As of the first quarter of 2015, Millennials became the largest generation in the workforce.[22] Their needs will influence businesses to think differently about how to engage employees and provide meaningful work and time for family, both of which are important to the Millennial generation. They are looking for more flexibility to make this all come together. And that helps all moms in the workplace, not only Millennial moms.

Millennials are also starting to become managers who will likely welcome different approaches to careers that offer more work-life balance, such as professional part-time work and remote or flexible work arrangements. As managers and decision-makers, they could also create the same for their teams or employees. Millennials can change the workforce based on their own interest in work-life balance, especially as they also start becoming moms and struggle with their own needs at work and home.

Generation X and Millennials Must Combine Efforts

I've broken down what makes these two generations of women in the workforce special. In reality, we need Gen X and Millennials working *together* to drive change in the workplace when it comes to work-life balance. Neither generation can do it alone. Instead of using an us-versus-them approach, let's combine efforts as women and working moms. Ultimately, we all want the same things; our approaches take us down different paths to get there. We can each play to our strengths so that we move the needle together. Doing so might make it happen faster and more easily.

In summary:

Changes are happening that impact moms in the US workforce.

- More companies are offering paid maternity leave.
- More working moms might want to stay engaged during the extremely important early development years.
- Moms with older children might want to spend more time with their kids to provide support or be engaged in activities.
- Working moms are being sandwiched between caring for their own families and their aging parents or parents-in-law.
- Generation X and Millennials must work together to make change happen in the workplace related to work-life balance.

CHAPTER 3

BENEFITS OF CHANGING YOUR APPROACH TO WORK-LIFE BALANCE

MOMS I TALKED TO SHARED THAT there was little time to do stuff when they weren't intentional with how they used their time. There is the rush to pick up kids after work, quickly prepare and then eat dinner, help with homework, bathe kids or clean up the kitchen while older kids bathe, and then get kids to bed. It's already been a long day at work and then all the other stuff. It's exhausting!

If you're using time like you always have, weekends are for catching up and doing the things that weren't done during the week, such as dropping off and picking up dry cleaning, grocery shopping, doing laundry, and cleaning the house. There might be kids' activities such as games or competitions. And there is even the need to help kids with school projects.

Moms shared much of the time as a family was getting things done, instead of enjoying the moment before they shifted their focus to more work-life balance. When was there time to even be able to create the moments as a family? When was there time to say "yes" to family fun?

Spending time together as a family is an integral part of what most moms want. We all want to create and enjoy the moments with our families, not work so hard and fly through those moments. Can you relate? Is this what you're going through now? The tips, tricks, and hacks I share won't magically make everything easy, but it will probably be easier for you to get more of what you want and give you more time to be the mom you want to be. A doctor of obstetrics and gynecology (OB-GYN) in Austin, Texas, shared, "It's never perfect, but it's doable."

More Time with Family

The number one benefit I heard in interviews was more time with family, whether attending activities or simply being home for dinner. (Not to mention time to make a healthy dinner.) It makes sense, though, right? The catalyst for thinking differently about your time management is often wanting to spend more time with your kids. More than half of moms I interviewed spe-cifically spoke about or alluded to the desire to spend more time with family.

In my case, when he was still an only child, I eventually wanted to be involved with our older son's school once he was in preschool. I wanted to be part of the fun activities and engage with his teachers. In the short-term, I wanted to attend mother and baby classes for things like music. It's hard to do those things with a typical approach to work-life balance.

What about Balance?

Let's talk about balance for a moment, since it's the topic I get the most questions about from working moms. Using your time different-ly can help you create more of the work-life balance you crave. About a quarter of moms mentioned balance as an end benefit. It seemed more like moms used balance to get more of what they wanted, especially time with kids. They didn't necessarily use balance as an end benefit in many cases, even when they mentioned the concept in our conversations.

The concept of balance is interesting and somewhat tricky. It's not something you can check off a list. You can't set it once and it's done. It's a constant shift in priorities—in your priorities—not those of anyone else. It looks different for each of us and that's OK.

I think of balance as more of a constantly moving pendulum that sways between work and family. Some days it swings more toward work and other days it's closer to family. It's constantly moving for me. Most moms I spoke with alluded to this shifting as well. The reality is that there is never (or almost never) a perfect fifty-fifty balance between family and work, which is natural and reasonable. Moms shouldn't be striving for something that is near impossible to achieve daily. If you look at balance over time it's more realistic. And the shift to a long-term approach–over a month, quarter, or even a year–instead of a daily goal is a mindset shift. It's a new way to think about balance, which might even help with the mommy guilt too.

More Flexibility

The number one key benefit specifically shared during the interviews was flexibility. A college counselor at a high school in Austin, Texas, described that flexibility gave her the ability to be more productive with her day.

And shifting your thinking on different aspects of work-life balance can give you more space and flexibility in general as you get more control of your time. The moms I interviewed were able to spend more time with kids because they controlled their schedule a bit more and controlled how they used their time instead of reacting to life and work demands.

Learning Something New

Learning a new skill or furthering their education came up a few times as a benefit when the working moms changed their approach to time. One physician in Austin, Texas, used her extra time to get a certificate in integrative and holistic medicine, a long-time area of interest. She wanted that additional education, so she could think differently about patient care.

Moms were able to start something new by understanding where they were spending their time, especially their time beyond the usual workweek. They would block out time or specifically schedule in the time to focus on something new. Several suggested delegating aspects of their lives, whether at work or home, at least in the short term, to start doing something new.

Motherhood and Personal Identity

We all love our families and truly enjoy the time we spend with our children and significant other and we also need our own identity. So many moms I interviewed talked about this, which isn't surprising considering the many high performing women I interviewed.

When I became a mother, the first year was so overwhelming. We were focused on our baby and almost nothing else, or that's how it felt. I remember waking up one morning around the time our older son turned one, looking in the mirror, and wondering what happened. Where had I gone? The woman I describe as before kids was different than the woman now looking at me in the mirror. I had been working for a large company at the time. I was trying to get through each day, not aiming to set goals for myself or trying to use my own natural rhythms. I wasn't focused on work-life balance; I was focusing on being a mom and the rest of me was temporarily lost.

This happened again, to a much lesser extent, when we had our younger son. The transition to two was incredibly tough in our house as we had a spirited, strong-willed, active toddler plus a newborn. This time I was working for myself, so I stepped away from my business for a few months to focus on our children and settling into a new rhythm. After a few months off, I started to do client work again and felt ready to make things happen. Plus, I had a first book to work on that I was excited about. I knew I didn't want to wake up one morning a year into having two children, wondering what happened yet again.

My work was an anchor for part of my identity outside of being a mother. I wanted to be more than a mom. I felt re-energized and stimulated mentally, even though I was exhausted physically when I was working. That something else is what kept me engaged in all areas of my life. It made me a better mom because I was confident and fulfilled in all the areas of my life.

I would have been able to find my own equilibrium more quickly if I had focused on work-life balance from the beginning with our older son. I would have been able to figure out that it's important for me to work, but it's also important for me to focus on self-care and life away from motherhood and work. I know I'm not alone in losing myself in motherhood and not focusing on my needs.

Passion Projects

The subject of passion projects came up over and over as an indirect benefit.

For some moms, these passion projects are an outlet. An information technology consultant in the beverage industry had a very demanding job before changing her approach to work-life balance. At one point, she even had to cancel a family vacation because of work demands. Now, in addition to more time with her own family, she has time to help families on their path to adoption. As the mother of adopted children, she feels passionately about helping other families on their adoption journey.

For others, these passion projects turn into a business over time. A director of digital marketing in New York City started her own coaching venture as a side business. Over time she started to focus more on her own business, which she is truly passionate about. This is now her sole focus. Would she even have pursued this new passion if she didn't use a different approach to work-life balance?

A woman's wellness coach, who helps moms figure out their own self-care needs, was a stay-at-home mom (SAHM) for about ten years. She had received a doctorate before taking time off when her first child was born. When her youngest of five children turned two, this self-care coach started getting antsy about going back to work. She started to think through what she wanted to do and found "her calling," as she describes it.

Benefit for Family

I was surprised by the many moms who talked about how these benefits trickled down to their families. The moms' focus on work-life balance impacted their kids and significant other. Maintaining their own identity made them better moms. Families benefitted from the moms' efforts on many levels, both directly and indirectly.

We don't talk about this aspect enough as working moms. I wanted to make sure to share this idea from the interviews, especially since there are statistics to back this up.

It turns out that about 59 percent of Americans think that one parent in a two-parent household should stay home to care for children, according to a 2016 Pew Research study.[1] The parent who stays home is usually the mother, although more dads are taking on this role, and more and more households have moms as the primary breadwinner. In case you're wondering, about 29 percent of partnered women are breadwinners in their families, according to a 2015 study done by Working Mother Research Institute.[2]

Although many Americans agree with this concept, a worldwide study shows it might be better for moms to work.[3] More than 13,000 women were part of this research, which found that daughters of working moms do better in the workforce over the long-term.[4] These daughters are more likely to have jobs, earn a higher wage, and have supervisory roles versus daughters of SAHMs.[5]

The same study with more than 13,000 women included more than 18,000 men and the impact on sons was different than that on daughters.[6] Men whose mothers worked are more likely to spend more time on family care duties than those whose mothers stayed at home.[7]

These findings may seem surprising to some, given so many Americans think moms should stay at home for the benefit of their children.

In summary:

Although focusing more on work-life balance doesn't make everything easy for moms, it will likely help you to get more of what you're looking for in your life.

- Moms in interviews mentioned more time with family, flexibility, balance, and time to try something new, to name a few.

- Families, not only moms, benefit from more work-life balance for moms.

- There is a long-term benefit to daughters and sons whose moms work.

PART II

WHAT TO CONSIDER BEFORE MAKING CHANGES IN YOUR WORK-LIFE BALANCE

CASE STUDY: Pivoting with Your Partner

This retail consultant is based near San Francisco and her path has had "twists and turns." She started out her career in the buying program at a large retailer. And after getting an MBA, her path took her to one of the biggest worldwide management consulting firms, where she had the opportunity to work on almost every major retailer imaginable.

She wanted to establish her roots and be in one place long enough to actually meet someone who she could spend her life with, so she went back to the retailer side for several years. During those years she got married and had her first child. While on maternity leave, the retail consultant decided it was time to make some changes and once again focus on work-life balance, but in a different way. She had kept in touch with senior leaders from her management consulting days and they asked her to join their new consulting firm. She worked with the team for seven years in a part-time role and, during that time, had her second child. And over time she transitioned to a full-time role for the past several years.

When talking about working for the smaller consulting firm, she shared it was a situation with mutual trust and mutual flexibility. They would give her the space she needed as a mom to two young children and she would dial into calls when she wasn't officially on the clock. She admits this was largely because they already knew her work product and work ethic. "If you know the people going into this, then there's mutual trust or, if you don't know each other, you must create a win-win when starting something new."

A few things factored into this retail consultant's decisions. In part she had a "conscious ebb and flow" because of life and professional events, such as the birth of a child or her husband starting a new coaching business. She and her husband look at both their career trajectories and one would pivot as the other's career took off. She and her husband are "100 percent of a partner for the other and one doesn't carry the mental load." It makes for a holistic approach to work-life balance for the two of them together. They absorb normal challenges that life throws their way and are able to focus on what's important. While it can be daunting to switch the "breadwinner" role in a relationship, things fall into place and the new routine emerges quickly.

Her advice for working moms looking for more work-life balance:

- *Know what resources you need.* She's had full-time help since her younger son was six months old. With both parents sometimes traveling, her family needed a nanny who felt empowered and in charge of the household. It's not simply taking care of kids. And the nannies and their roles have changed over time.

- *Outsource responsibilities, not just tasks.* It can be hard to let go, especially if you're a Type A personality or more controlling by nature. It's freeing when you finally let go of the full mental load and responsibility, though.

- *Keep in touch with your network.* When it comes to networking, "do what's natural" to you. Understand the importance of work "friendships" and build on those, even when you don't work together any more. Send a birthday message or share an article of interest.

CHAPTER 4

IS YOUR EMPLOYER HELPING OR HURTING YOUR WORK-LIFE BALANCE?

WHEN LOOKING AT LONG-TERM opportunities with a company where you feel supported and grow professionally in the short and long term, look at the company and the industry culture before taking a specific path or starting a job. Do your homework on the company and industry. For example, look on the company or industry group websites or even at a company's online reviews from current and previous employees. Check out **www.mompowerment.com** for an updated list of websites that provide this type of information.

These resources help potential employees understand policies versus practice because they might be different. Look for articles and read the reviews from current and former employees or, better yet, speak to current and former employees about how policies and culture influence behavior as it relates to work-life balance. You can find alumni from your university or ask people in your own network for contacts at the company or in the industry. Start having those tough conversations, even before you are in an interview.

If you're already at a company, start talking to women in senior roles. Understand their path at the company. What, if anything, did they have to sacrifice to get to where they are? Look for any groups that help support women within the company. Find out about work-life balance initiatives or programs in place for when mothers come back from maternity leave. Talk to women in other departments or on different teams because the path and support might vary from department to department or from one team to another. Understand everything your employer offers and start taking advantage of those programs.

Culture and Norms: Industry versus Company

When you're looking at current and future opportunities, take time to understand specific company and industry norms, which can dramatically impact work-life balance. Moms from all sorts of industries contributed to this book with their advice, insights, and stories. Some moms shared that their industry enables moms to maintain greater work-life balance. Others mentioned that work-life balance was hard to create. Some even started their own business to create the work-life balance they were looking for.

The culture and norms of an industry help enable or deter you from changing how you approach different aspects of work-life balance such as productivity. And then sometimes it is a specific company's approach or policies that made a difference to the moms who shared their stories. The industry and company cultures work together to empower moms to make changes or take away the power to make these changes.

For example, I spoke with several moms who are social workers. One of these moms in Michigan explained that she gets support from her employer because the organization is dedicated to good relationships with parents. She described her employer as "a great place for her with a young child, because of the culture of the organization and the high level of flexibility." The organization specifically works with young children and their parents, and the company treats its employees the same way it does its clients.

Many of the moms I interviewed are in industries not necessarily known for their flexibility. One of these industries is healthcare. Several moms are medical providers, specifically either some sort of doctor or dentist. The two dentists, both in Austin, Texas, shared that more work-life balance was part of the reason for going into that side of the medical field. Before they even started graduate school, they knew they wanted to enter healthcare and specifically chose dentistry for the long-term opportunity for work-life balance versus going into a medical field with long hours.

The moms who work as doctors shared that the medical profession is not usually supportive of work-life balance. In fact, a few of the moms worked in academic roles within medicine to achieve the work-life balance they were looking for. I spoke with an OB-GYN in Austin, Texas, who created a job share situation in a private practice. She and another doctor act as one doctor, with the same approach to patient care, each working part time. In this situation, part time is thirty to forty hours per week in comparison to full time, which is sixty or more hours per week.

That said, I spoke with moms in industries known for a lack of work-life balance such as finance, technology, and public accounting. I chatted with a chief financial officer of a small hedge fund in the New York City area. She mentioned she could work for a larger hedge fund with even more responsibility and complexity to her role, but she likely wouldn't be able to have the work-life balance she currently does. She is an exception, but I mention her situation because even in the most demanding industries and careers, you can still find or create work-life balance.

The moms in technology and public accounting who shared

their stories with me needed to create change in their lives. They had worked for several years for their employers and knew their own value. One mom who works for a large technology company needed to make a change because her kids were getting older and their activities were ramping up. She took a three-month sabbatical and when she came back, she was more focused on project-based work as she created more work-life balance built in to her approach to work.

There are some companies willing to make major changes to keep high-performing employees at the company. One of these companies was in the petrochemical industry. I wouldn't have initially considered this company or industry as work-life balance friendly. Part of the reason behind this flexibility was based on the moms being high performers. These companies didn't want to lose highly valuable team members who were willing to leave the workforce altogether if they couldn't find more work-life balance. And, it's not uncommon for these large petrochemical companies to have diversity initiatives in place to attract top talent, regardless of gender or race. They're looking to keep these employees at the company over the long term.

There are companies and industries that don't have these types of policies in place. Of the moms I interviewed, almost 40 percent are entrepreneurs, many of whom started a company because they couldn't find the right work-life balance in the company where they worked or at other companies within their industry. I dedicate Chapter 9 to those who are considering entrepreneurship because their needs are a bit different than those working moms who are employed, whether at a small business or multinational corporation.

What to Look for in an Employer

For those moms who want to continue to work for a company and not go the entrepreneur route, I understand where you're coming from. My first year as a working mother was at a large company where I had worked for about five and a half years.

If you're looking at your current employer or at other companies and you want to be at that company for the long term, you want to make sure it's the right fit for your needs over time, right? Based on the interviews I did and on further research, there are five areas that seem to impact moms over the long term at a company, beyond specific job duties. Understanding these areas can help you find employers who are interested in the long-term growth of female employees and who understand that a woman's needs change over time.

Flexibility

One key concept is flexibility. If a company is interested in empowering employees to have work-life balance, it needs to provide employees with a level of flexibility. Perhaps your child is at home sick and you need to work from home for a day or two. Or maybe you have someone coming to your home to fix an appliance or install new equipment. What if you need to accompany your own mom to doctor appointments if her health is starting to deteriorate? Can you work from home or leave early? Is flexibility something the CEO talks about, but it's not actually used further down the ranks? You want an employer that not only has these policies and talks about them, but also empowers employees to use them. Each time shouldn't require a favor from your manager. You want managers to be supportive upfront and not engage human resources (HR) to take advantage of existing policy. (Keep in mind that HR might get involved to execute a long-term plan you agree on with your manager.)

A makeup artist in Austin, Texas, shared, "I feel I can say no to opportunities when they conflict with family obligations or family time." She can decline to work on a project or at an event and it won't impact her career. In her situation, part of the reason for flexibility is because her manager is also a mom. When you look for flexibility in a company, it's about empowering managers to allow for flexibility in dealing with their employees, as well as a level of flexibility that employees naturally have in any role. What happens if her manager changed? Would the company still provide that level of flexibility or was it an understanding manager who empowered employees?

If you're not sure which of these situations it is, ask around. Talk to other women who don't work for your same manager. Talk to employees in other departments and hear about their experiences and situations. Is it a series of one-off agreements or is it company policy?

Non-Traditional Work and Schedule Options (or Openness to Options)

Several moms who shared their story with me are engineers at a large multinational petrochemical company based in Houston, Texas. These employees are well-trained, have years of experience, and are high performing. In addition, the company has diversity initiatives and programs to keep women moving through different departments and up the ranks. These moms might have moved from one team or department to another when they wanted more control over or flexibility in their schedules. The company is open to empowering employees to make changes in what their workday looks like.

A Connecticut-based mom in media sales shared that she gets support from her employer because the focus is on meeting goals, not on hours. In her situation, she doesn't have to be in the office to achieve her goals.

What about in the situations where you are the first employee to try to focus on work-life balance? Even if everyone has a traditional approach to time management, you want upper management and the company overall to be open to the possibility.

When a Chicago-based attorney initially approached her employer about changing up her work week, the response was for her to "figure out what you need" and the company would support it. Her employer didn't want to lose her and was willing to be incredibly flexible to keep her from leaving.

Work-life Balance Initiatives

Most companies, big or small, have some sort of benefits. The most basic is health benefits. What about work-life balance initiatives though? What other benefits does the company pay for, such as gym membership or backup childcare? For moms who have recently had a baby, how does the company support or facilitate pumping (e.g., provide a dedicated, comfortable area for moms to pump, encourage pumping instead of treating it as an inconvenience, etc.)? What else does the company do to enable its employees to have more work-life balance?

What about work-life balance initiatives for those who aren't parents? Does the company give a paid (or even partially paid) sabbatical to employees, regardless of whether they are parents or not? Do employees actually use this benefit? What happens after they return from their sabbatical? For most people I know whose companies provide a sabbatical to employees after a certain number of years of service, they must stay for a specific amount of time after taking the sabbatical. If that's the case with your employer or the company you're considering, what happens after that time limit is up? If most employees leave, that might not be the best sign.

Let's be honest, it doesn't help to have work-life balance opportunities in place for show. So, how do they feel about you actually using those work-life balance tools and services? It's great to have initiatives in place, but it won't make a difference if it's frowned upon, should you choose to use them.

And it's helpful to see that work-life balance initiatives are actually based on input from employees. If the company pays for gym memberships but no one uses them, why does the company have that benefit? If you see other areas where you'd like support like back-up childcare, bring together a group of working parents to make the request to support that. Most companies that provide this benefit either pay for a certain number of hours of back-up care or pay for the fee to join this kind of resource and supplement that cost. For example, if it's usually $15 per hour for a babysitter, it will only cost you $5 per hour. That's a big difference over the course of a year. And it takes stress off of the situation of those unexpected times when your usual childcare falls through.

Career Growth for all Female Employees

Do women where you work seem to change trajectory once they become mothers to the dreaded "mommy track?" Are there mothers working throughout the company at more senior levels? What has their career path looked like over time?

How many women are there in senior leadership roles, regardless of if they are moms or not? What career paths have they followed? If they've had to claw their way to the top, fighting for every promotion, even though they were qualified, that might not be the best environment for supporting working moms. And for that matter, look at the company's board. Are there women? Look at what types of initiatives they might be involved with. See if the company publicly talks about creating more opportunities for engaging women at more senior levels and see if that's actually happening.

A media director at a large marketing agency in Austin, Texas, transitioned to smaller pieces of business instead of the larger, more demanding clients when she made some changes to her work-life balance. In addition, the company focused her more on East Coast clients instead of West Coast clients, which was more in line with her schedule needs. It would have been too hard to keep this marketing mom on large accounts with 24/7 demands. Her clients have changed, but she still has a meaningful role on smaller accounts with important needs.

An online media editor talked about how she wouldn't have grown professionally at her previous employer. She would have been in the "back seat," couldn't have taken on a bigger role, and would have worked more hours. In addition, the role would have been writing only, which would have limited her long-term career options. The difference with her current employer is that the culture allows for several career paths specifically designed with flexibility in mind for working moms. In addition, everyone works from home at her current employer. The woman who started the online publication worked for a major publication and then got pregnant, so she created an environment with a lot more work-life balance and flexibility for employees since it was what she also wanted.

Several of the engineers I spoke with at the multinational petrochemical company based out of Houston described a willingness from the company and from their managers to move the moms to other opportunities that made more sense for greater flexibility. There are several options and positions to choose from. It depended on the mom's current skills, what skills she wanted to build, and what kind of work the mom wanted to do, in addition to the number of hours she wanted to work.

Maternity Policy

When you're a professional working mom, work-life balance can begin with maternity leave. Although the focus of my book is on what happens after maternity leave, I want to take a moment to discuss maternity leave itself. From a business perspective, there are a few elements to keep in mind when an employee wants to have a baby. Look at all sides to really understand the company's maternity leave policy.

First, there is the legal side of things. The federal law that keeps companies from firing the women who take time off to have a baby is the Family and Medical Leave Act (FMLA). If you haven't yet had a child or dealt with major illness, you might not be familiar with FMLA. This is the law that requires US employers to provide their employees with job protection and unpaid leave for up to twelve weeks once each 365 days for qualified family and medical reasons (e.g., having a baby or because of a major illness), whether yours or someone in your immediate family (e.g., your child, parent, spouse, etc.). You cannot lose your job unless the position is eliminated (i.e., no one will have the job because it no longer exists).

It's important to note that not all companies must comply with federal FMLA requirements. Companies with fifty or more employees within a seventy-five-mile radius of the office must comply with this law. And if you work for the local, state, or federal government or a public or private school, you are eligible for FMLA as long as you've been with the company for at least twelve months. Those twelve months don't have to be a consecutive, but they must have happened within the past seven years. And, an added requirement is that employees must work at least 1,250 hours during those twelve months. Essentially, some part-time employees might not be eligible. When you break it down, employees who have worked more than twenty-four hours per week over those twelve months are eligible.

Even with recent hires, some companies still choose to follow FMLA guidelines. Some small businesses don't have to follow the FMLA guidelines, but they do it anyway because work-life balance matters to them. And, let's be honest, it's a great way to attract top talent who might have been interested in working for a larger company.

Second, there is the issue of paid or unpaid maternity leave. At the time this book was written, maternity leave policy in the business world and at the government level in the United States was getting more attention, but the overall approach in the US is not even in the same league as other developed nations. The United States is the only developed nation in the world that doesn't provide paid maternity leave at a national level. As a point of comparison, most other developed nations provide anywhere from six months to more than a year of maternity leave that is paid at full or partial salary. In fact, according to an analysis of the top sixty employers done by a nonprofit that advocates for paid family leave, the Paid Leave for the United States (PL+US), and Global Health Vision, "the majority of the top employers in the U.S. offer no paid family leave or are not transparent about their paid family leave policy."[1]

Why does it matter if it's paid or not? Imagine not receiving a salary for four, six, or sixteen weeks while you're taking care of a new member of your family. Most families can't take unpaid maternity leave for an extended time because of the financial implications. They can't afford it.

Another interesting element is that a company might not pay salary in the normal way during maternity leave. In my situation, my maternity leave was paid through short-term disability and I received eight weeks off instead of the usual six because I had a Caesarian section (C-section). I took an additional four weeks that was a combination of sick time and vacation days to have a total of twelve weeks of paid maternity. That basically wiped out my vacation for the rest of the year. The challenge is that when it comes to short-term disability and other ways to pay out maternity leave, it's inconsistent since policies can vary from state to state.

You might be wondering why maternity leave matters. Companies are starting to recognize the need for paid time off after having a baby. Giving birth isn't usually easy work and don't forget that a C-section is major surgery. Maternity leave helps moms allow their bodies to heal, form a stronger bond with baby, and even get babies into a rhythm, which is hard to do when baby is a month old. These are integral to helping moms get back to work, able to focus, and be at peak productivity during work hours after maternity leave.

And, finally, there is the issue of how work will happen when a mother is out on maternity leave, which could be weeks or months. Does your work stop for the time you're gone, so that you come back to what seems like a mountain of work and you're forever catching up? Is the work divided among your team or colleagues, so that your role is covered through others? Maybe they hire someone temporarily while you're out on maternity leave. Does the approach vary from manager to manager or by department? Ask around to see what happens because this might provide some interesting insights into how they value their female team members and how they help re-integrate them back into work once they return from maternity leave.

Some companies provide part-time opportunities as moms get back from maternity leave with limited, if any, travel, in addition to services specifically for these moms. Their reentry is gradual. More companies are starting to offer this reentry approach as moms come back from maternity leave in efforts to keep moms from leaving the workforce.[2] Especially in highly competitive industries where companies invest heavily in their employees, companies want to ensure moms return after maternity leave.[3]

The general and specific information on maternity leave can be complicated and difficult to understand, so make sure to do some digging using all sorts of resources, including conversations with moms at the company. You might be able to find moms to talk to through the alumni group at your alma mater or through your own network. And consider the maternity policy and how current moms use that policy. Does the website or employee manual say twelve weeks, but no one takes more than six because everyone is asked to come back early? Look on **www.mompowerment.com** for links to resources that have more information on maternity policies.

In summary:

There are many aspects of a job and industry that can impact your work-life balance.

- Consider the cultural norms in the industry and at the employer to understand policies versus how they are implemented.

- Understand what kinds of flexibility companies provide to employees and what work-life balance initiatives are in place.

- Take time to look at career path opportunities and overall growth opportunities.

- Consider what flexibility exists for employees and the general openness to non-traditional career model, even if the positions don't currently exist.

- Look into maternity policy at the company.

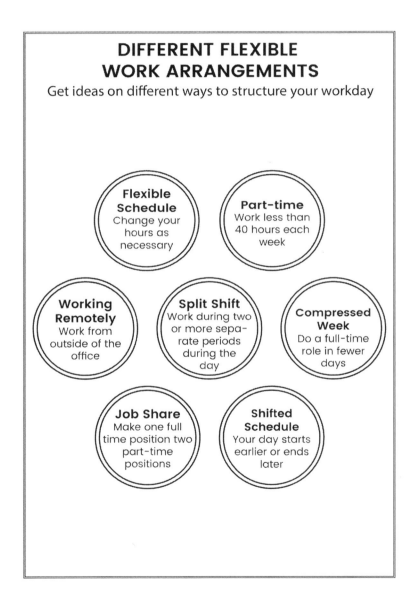

CHAPTER 5

UNDERSTAND YOUR MOTIVATION FOR CHANGE

Now that we understand some things in your environment that can impact your work-life balance, let's move on to figuring out the motivation behind wanting to change your work-life balance.

As you go through this section, you might find it helpful to talk through it with someone. Reach out to a trusted colleague at work who might be in the same situation. Ask your significant other to talk through it with you. Consider talking to a friend, sibling, parent, etc. Or it might be beneficial to reach out to a trusted career advisor. This can be the foundation to next steps, so talk to whomever can help you better understand your feelings about and perspective on your work situation.

First, figure out your motivation because your motivation becomes your guide as you make changes. You want to make sure you're getting out of this new scenario what you're seeking. And, once you understand this, you'll understand what is motivating you and what you want your time to look like.

For example, maybe you want to spend time with an aging, sick parent. Are there appointments that you'd like to be present for? Will that require more flexibility in your day so you need to figure out how to be more productive throughout? Or do you need to figure out how to make the appointments more consistently in the morning so that it's more predictable and you arrive a bit late to the office on specific days of the week?

Second, understanding your motivation helps you with matching what things you need to add and take away to get you the work-life balance you're looking for. What do you need to change in order to volunteer at your daughter's school every other week for forty-five minutes? What things do you need to change around to attend the creative writing class you've been wanting to try for years?

And finally, when you've thought through your motivation, you're better able to sell the changes you're looking to make to your manager or senior management. It's helpful to brainstorm a bit by yourself or even with a friend who understands what needs to be done and can help you think outside of the box.

Maybe what you figure out as you look at your motivation is that this is the time to pivot into a new career or to start your own business. If you don't take the time to understand your why, you won't know that you might need to make bigger changes.

How to Figure Out Your Motivation

I worked in large marketing agencies for more than twelve years before focusing 100 percent on my own business. Not everyone realizes it, but working at a marketing agency can be very demanding. On a good week, I worked fifty-five hours.

After working at various marketing agencies for more than five years, I wanted my life back. I decided to take things into my own hands and went to graduate school for my MBA. I knew I wanted more work-life balance and I thought making a career shift was the right answer. What I really wanted was an employer and a job that enabled that work-life balance. I wanted to be strategic and an integral part of a team, but I didn't want to travel a bunch or be needed 24/7.

After grad school, I found that balance at the large marketing agency where I worked for six and a half years. About a year after becoming a mom, I focused only on my strategic marketing consulting business, which I had done as a side hustle for about eight years at that point.

My own version of work-life balance enables me to be the face my boys see at the end of their day. I want them to know I am always there for them, to celebrate something they're proud of and provide support on not-so-great days. That interaction with my boys is important to me and important to them.

I volunteer and attend events at their schools. I'm able to be engaged with other parents in their school and truly be part of those school communities.

You might be reading this and say "I want more of that" or "I need a change" and yet not be able to articulate the motivation behind it. You now know it's important to understand your "why," but how do you uncover it in your own situation?

Figuring out your motivation takes some soul searching and self-reflection. The questions I'm including will help you figure out your own motivation for wanting to make changes in your approach to balance and maybe even lead you to ask your own questions that uncover even more behind your motivation.

Ask "Why?"

It's helpful to ask, "Why do I want this change?" That might sound simple, but there is a bit more to it. You know your motivation (e.g., spending time with your kids), but what is the "why" behind that? Drill down a bit more to understand the underlying motivation and not what is at the surface. Ask "why" a few times to start figuring out the real answer behind your motivation. You might be surprised at what you uncover.

What Do You Want to Change?

Now that you're starting to understand why you want to make changes, what is it that you want to change? Try to be specific. Don't simply say, "I want more work-life balance." Understanding the "what" will help you make adjustments, big or small, that align with what you want to change. For example, do you want to start later at the office and make up the time at home later so you can drop off your child at school? Can you start your day earlier after dropping off your child at school and leave earlier so you can attend his or her activities more regularly?

What does it Look Like?

It's helpful to do some brainstorming on what these changes look like in the best case. It might also help to visualize what you want and try to describe the scene or picture in your mind. That might help you think through and put words to what you want. Think about the elements that you want to include and consider what must be included (i.e., your non-negotiables). Now that you understand what it looks like, you can use that visual as part of your plan when you speak with your manager, your significant other, and your family.

And remember that there are multiple aspects to this: your family (significant other and your children), your professional life, you and what you personally need, maybe extended family (e.g., your mom and dad and siblings), friends, neighbors, and even colleagues.

Time for Career Change or Pivot

Are you still excited about your career? You might not be excited about your job, but are you still excited about what you generally do? You know you want a change, but you enjoy what you do.

Are you still happy with the company you work for? If the answer is yes, but you're still feeling hesitant, maybe you need to see what is available on other teams or in other departments. Talk to people about their experience with a different manager, on another team, or in a department outside of your own.

If the answer is "not very excited" when you start thinking through your enthusiasm about the company you work for, perhaps it's time to look at other companies and leave your current employer. Consider if there are other companies in the same industry or even related industries that provide more of what you're looking for. Understanding your motivation will help you figure out which companies are a good fit and which ones to avoid.

Or maybe it's time for a career pivot where you use your skills in a very different capacity. This is a different conversation that you might want to have with your significant other, friends, colleagues, or a career coach to see if you need to make changes to better align you for something new.

If you're unhappy with your company or industry overall, is part of what's driving your motivation a desire to become an entrepreneur instead of working for someone else? Is it time to manage your own business? Don't take this leap lightly. Being an entrepreneur is not easy, but it does put you in the driver's seat on your hours, growth, and even types of projects and clients. Is this the change you're looking for?

For almost 40 percent of moms I interviewed this was the case. They couldn't find what they were looking for at a company, so they started their own business. They control when they work, how many hours, who they work with (this becomes even more the case as they became more seasoned entrepreneurs), and even which days or hours they work. Most agree that it's not easy though. It takes a lot of work. More on that in Chapter 9.

In summary:

Understanding your motivation is a key element to making changes to your work-life balance.

- Understand why you're interested in making changes.

- Visualize what changes look like.

- Take time to uncover if you need to make shifts in your career or employer, or if it's time to focus on starting your own business.

CHAPTER 6

YOUR SIGNIFICANT OTHER AND WORK-LIFE BALANCE

WE'VE TALKED ABOUT FINDING SUPPORT from your employer and being in an industry with all sorts of empowerment and initiatives for working moms. What about getting support from your significant other on the home front?

Is Your Significant Other Helping or Hurting Your Work-life Balance?

When you're trying to make changes in your work-life balance, it's not only about changes at work or changes you can make yourself. Let's face it, when we're in a committed relationship, we need and want the support of our significant other as we make these changes. How is your significant other supporting these changes? (Consider letting your significant other read this chapter or at least discussing what we cover, even if you don't go through the questions.)

I heard over and over in the interviews about moms managing the lion's share of both childcare and household duties—about 75 percent of moms I spoke with said this. I did hear about an equal or near equal split of duties in the other roughly 25 percent. And, while I don't have an equal split of duties in my own household, my husband does take on certain tasks (we'll get more into that later). Take a moment to consider how duties fall in your household.

How can you divide chores or tasks more fairly? In my family's case, my husband and I divide the childcare and household duties most evenings. Whoever puts the kids to bed doesn't do dishes. It's helpful because it doesn't squarely put either of those duties on any-one person's shoulders. And while some of you might say that put-ting kids to bed isn't bad, you have forgotten how tough it can be to brush a preschooler's teeth every night. And besides, if you clean up the kitchen plus put kids to bed, we're talking hours of time and I often use the evening hours to get a bit more work done and to get ready for the next day. It also happens to be a great example for our boys that both mom and dad divide duties in our home.

You can divide up other duties specifically related to your chil-dren. For example, whoever drops kids off at school or day care doesn't have to pick up. That way one parent can get into the office earlier. Whoever naturally works later can do drop off, so kids still get mommy or daddy time in the morning and that parent can be engaged, even when working late. Plus, it gives the other parent the chance to start earlier at the office to give a bit more mental space or even to essentially shift hours a bit earlier which likely allows that parent to leave work a bit earlier as well.

The idea in both of these is that one parent isn't responsible for everything related to household chores or tasks related to childcare.

The Mental Load

Even if your significant other is taking on an actual duty, are you still managing it? For most moms, the answer is yes. And this takes on another layer of work. We first heard about elements of the mental load in Arlie Hochschild's book, _The Second Shift: Working Families and_ the Revolution at Home in 1989. Moms essentially manage all the stuff at home on top of their workload at the office (e.g., babysitter, house-keeper, running grocery list, summer camp, buying new clothes for kids when they outgrow old clothes, etc.). On top of whatever child-care and household duties you have, are you also managing the mental load of everything related to your family and household?

In my case, my husband does most of the cooking since I needed some things off of my plate and he felt confident in this task. He did this in the first year of each of our boys' lives. I'm not sure we would have survived without his excellent cooking skills. Until recently, I decided the menu for the week, created the shopping list, and often did the prep. My husband did the actual cooking each night, though. I realized that I couldn't take this approach anymore because it actually saved me very little time. So, now he's in charge of the menu planning for the week, meal prep, cooking, and making any adjustments necessary throughout the process. I can run to the store occasionally, but it's generally his thing now. The idea was to shift the whole mental load of meals to him instead of me having it and him simply executing my plan.

Men are totally capable at work and they can be equally capable at home. I don't know about you, but the last time I went out of town, I left a detailed itinerary of schedules, activities that they could do on the weekend and regular activities on weekdays, food in the freezer, etc. Looking back, I realized that, other than making sure he had times correct for pick-up, he would have done fine if I hadn't left the other instructions. He could have figured it out. I understand this is the case with my husband, who is parenting our seven- and four-and-a-half-year-olds. It might look a bit different when parenting a baby or toddler. If you're a mom who is fully engaged with her child and knows all his or her likes, dislikes, etc., you will likely need to provide more direction. I almost wonder if this might be the case again when kids are teenagers. The idea, though, is that dads will figure it out, so let's let them do just that. Figure it out.

Time to Let Go?

For me, I've learned to be specific with my husband when I want things done a certain way. When that's not the case, I must be comfortable with it being done and know it won't necessarily be my way. As someone who likes to be in control and can be particular with how she likes things, that is a huge mindset shift.

In our case, dinner might look a bit different than I would make it. Our go-to meals will change. Our kids will also be exposed to different types of cuisine and ingredients than my usual staples. There is nothing wrong with that, as long as the meals are healthy, filling, and tasty.

Is this something you're ready for? If not, what can you do to take small steps to get mentally prepared for some of these changes?

Can Anything Go Away?

I'll speak more about outsourcing later, but are there tasks or duties that can go away? Essentially, you won't outsource them and no one in your house will do them either. Be creative with how you look at things.

When my older son was in mothers' day out and preschool, I attended every party that I could. All the moms did, regardless of whether or not we worked. I've changed this approach for my younger son. This past school year in his pre-school class, we agreed early on in the school year as a group of moms that we wouldn't attend every event. We would only attend when we were the moms assigned to the particular class party (e.g., Halloween or Easter). Talk about removing the pressure. All of us breathed a sigh of relief and gained hours of time over the school year. We united and figured it out together instead of feeling we must do this because we had in the past. Empowered working motherhood at its best!

Do I Need to do All the Things Myself?

I get that as mothers we want to attend everything that our kids do and engage in all the special activities—the school performances, the dance recitals, the random class visits, volunteer time in the classroom, etc. The list is endless, right?

What if you shared those duties with your significant other? We shouldn't feel that we are required to attend everything while working forty-plus hours each week. Let's empower our significant others to attend those events and do those volunteer opportunities. Think about the load off your shoulders to know that your significant other could attend some events and activities that you normally would. Think of what a great example your husband could be to other dads and even to your children to see a dad engaged with the activities and opportunities that are usually designated for mom.

If you are caring for an aging parent or in-law, is this something your significant other can take on? How can your significant other take over responsibilities such as scheduling and attending medical or specialist appointments or visiting the family member at his or her home or care facility?

Conversation with Your Significant Other

If you have read this chapter and realized that you'd like to change things between you and your partner, it might be time for a conversation. I've included some questions for you and your significant other to talk through for this very topic. That way you're able to create more of the work-life balance you're craving and you can empower your significant other along the way.

- What is each parent in charge of now?

- How did you choose these tasks?

- How does each person play to his or her strengths?

- What are the types of changes you are expecting related to the different duties for both parents?

- What are your thoughts on expectations from both you and your significant other? What are your partner's expectations?

- What kind of support do you want and need from your significant other?

- What direction, support, etc. does your significant other need from you to be empowered to help with a task?

- What are you each really good at that you can take over related to household or childcare duties?

- What tasks or chores does each of you want to avoid? Do you have the ability to outsource that task? If not, how will you trade off so that it doesn't fall squarely on one parent's shoulders?

- What ground rules should there be on what happens when a child is sick or sent home from school?

- How can your significant other help with chores so that mom can fit in more self-care, whatever that looks like?

- What are the types of activities you would each like to engage with for the kids?

- What coverage do you need for tasks related to caring for an aging relative, if any? How can each of you share tasks or duties here?
- How do you coordinate all the activities together?
- What type of help are you looking at from outside the home?

See the template on **www.mompowerment.com** to help you prepare before and take notes during the conversation(s) with your significant other.

In summary:

To achieve better work-life balance, see if you're getting the right level of support at home.

- Look at which household or childcare duties you can divide differently.
- Consider how your significant other can help with your mental load.
- Are there specific duties or tasks that can simply go away, so that no one inside or outside of your home needs to do them?
- What are the activities that your significant other can attend or participate in instead of you?
- Discuss what changes you'd like to make in how you partner in caring for your family and taking care of all the things that must be done.

PART III

SETTING YOURSELF UP TO SUCCEED

CASE STUDY: What Happens when Life at Home Changes

The Atlanta-based information technology (IT) consultant had worked for sixteen years in various operations roles in media companies and somewhere in there, took a break to do a two-year MBA. Her roles within the media industry were demanding; so much so that at one point, she had to cancel a family vacation. And that led her to considering other industries.

She found a great role at a major beverage company, but things at home changed. The IT professional realized she needed to spend more time with her then young daughter. She eventually found a home with a consulting group she had collaborated with while employed by the beverage company. She had spoken to their leadership team while they were doing consulting work at her then current employer. Once she decided to join their team, she was working on projects at her previous employer with someone she knew who knew her and her skills. The biggest benefit of that was that she could do great work, but it wasn't all-consuming and she didn't have to prove herself with a new team.

For a few years, the big difference was that she worked less than half the hours she had worked while full-time and made about the same salary. The IT consultant had time with her family at home and at her children's school. She shared about how much better her family's quality of life was during that time. And she had time for passion projects, like helping people with their adoption journey.

Since doing the original interview a few years ago, this IT expert has returned to full-time work with a wider scope of responsibility. She is working at the same company that was her client when she was a part-time consultant. This time the shift came from circumstances changing at work. She still has flexibility—both the opportunity to work from home and flexible hours. Part of this flexibility stems from not having to start from scratch to rebuild her personal brand with a team. The team knew the IT professional, her abilities, and general work ethic. She is still able to carve out the necessary time for her family and other outside demands.

Her advice for anyone interested in more work-life balance:

- *Keep up your network.* Maintain relationships because you never know where those relationships will lead down the road. Her work opportunities have all come from being engaged with her network and being open to new conversations with people she knows.

- *Create a win-win scenario.* You want situations to be mutually beneficial. Know what your team and senior leadership need. Be aware of what you and your family need and ask for those things.

- *Don't make hasty decisions.* Take your time making decisions, both when looking at a transition and during the actual transition.

- *Work to mutual needs.* It matters what others need, not just what you need. Especially when you're looking for more flexibility and work-life balance in general, consider both your personal needs and those of your team and employer.

CHAPTER 7

NETWORKING SMARTER

IF YOU'RE READING THIS BOOK, chances are you're looking to make changes at work and/or home to help you have better work-life balance. As part of this change, you may consider a new role at your current employer or a competitor. And that is where networking comes in. Networking is the most discussed topic and piece of advice from more than 110 interviews, with about 30 percent of the moms giving this advice. Whether you want to change roles where you're currently employed, change companies, or create your own board of directors (more on that in the next chapter), networking will help.

And networking even helped the 38 percent of moms who started their own businesses. Their new businesses were usually in the same industry where they had been previously employed, so they needed to maintain their contacts. Their network could be potential customers or could open doors and make connections with potential customers.

So, the question becomes: How do you make the most of your limited time and squeeze in networking? You want to make the most of your limited time, right?

Networking as Intentional Interactions

When you hear the word "networking," you might think of large networking events where there is a lot of exchanging business cards. These can be industry events with a focus on specific topic or panels with industry experts. You often pay a hefty price for a ticket to attend. Maybe your employer sends you to these events to network with potential customers and suppliers or to hear more from your counterparts at your competitors. They might be close by and happen for an evening or a whole day. What about when they last several days, taking you away from family and changing up your family's routine? For some, this is a blessing and something they look forward to, but for many moms this is an inconvenience, even with all the benefits to your career.

From an online perspective, networking might make you think of the many seemingly random requests from people to join your online networks. How did they even find you, you might sometimes wonder? (At least I sometimes wonder that.)

The larger networking opportunities and the blindly reaching out or accepting online requests to join a network may or may not help you. What will? Most moms talked about focused efforts, although having lots of touch points was certainly helpful to some moms.

A senior engineer at a large multinational petrochemical company in Houston, Texas, shared that she does intentional networking. She doesn't have time for a random lunch with a coworker, but she intentionally makes time to meet with coworkers and industry colleagues at lunch once a week or every few weeks. That conversation and interaction serve a purpose. This engineer prepares for these interactions and knows what she wants to cover so that she can make the most of her limited time.

Have a Networking Plan

These intentional interactions get you closer to your short-term and long-term career goals. To be the most prepared, create a plan. You can include what makes sense. If you're specifically looking to talk to internal colleagues, your plan will look different than if you're looking for a new job outside of your company or industry.

Elements to consider for your plan

- Keep in touch with your current network, both online and in person.

- Create goals on who to contact, number of contacts to make, or even what types of connections you want to make. Hint: give yourself deadlines to make sure you stay on target with your efforts.

- Define what you are looking for in your conversations (e.g., meeting people and extending your initial touchpoints, understanding a different company or industry perspective).

- Articulate your "ask" at the end of the networking session, if you plan on having this as part of your networking interaction. Hint: Make sure that you don't force your agenda and your needs if it's not natural to the conversation. Maybe this is an initial conversation and another time you do more of the networking side of things with an "ask." Only you will be able to gauge this from the interaction.

- Know what you want to offer in return for whatever you're asking. And it can be as simple as asking "What can I help you with?"

Network Where You Are

Now that you're thinking about who to meet with, where do you find them? Do you attend those large industry events where hundreds or thousands of industry people come together for speakers and panels? They are great from a learning perspective and you can meet a lot of people who you might not have access to every day. You can even get access to industry experts who might be a keynote or a panel participant. On the other hand, they can also be expensive and time consuming, and the contacts you make might or might not be meaningful, based on your networking goals and skills. Remember, you're aiming for intentional networking.

Let's say you attend one or two larger events a year, what about the rest of the year? Or what if attending a large event isn't something you can work in right now?

My suggestion is to network where you are. That way you have productive and meaningful conversations in more intimate settings on a more regular basis. There are five places to consider for networking where you are:

- Meet with colleagues at your current employer in an informal setting
- Network online
- Network with parents from your child's school
- Get to know your neighbors
- Chat with new people at social gatherings you're attending

Talking to Someone at Your Current Employer

If you work for an employer, what about the built-in network of your colleagues? When was the last time you spent time with a colleague who you don't usually work with to hear what he or she does within his or her team or department? Probably not recently, if ever. In addition, most colleagues have worked somewhere else. Get to know these current colleagues and their stories in an informal setting like lunch or coffee and you can steer the conversation to learn more about their current and past roles and employers or any organizations he or she might be involved with.

You can also find out about their previous roles and initiatives in which they were involved. Whether they are more senior, your peer, or someone more junior, you can approach the conversation as a learning opportunity to better understand what's going on at the company and what they have achieved on their path at your employer, which is likely different from yours. You can learn about different managers, departments, initiatives, and even different locations. Networking is an easy way to ask about what teams or other departments are working on and learn more about positions that offer more work-life balance.

For example, what if you're a petrochemical engineer on a global team that has ongoing needs where you must be in the office daily. You're looking for more flexibility and are wanting an opportunity where you can work from home one day a week. If changing things around won't work on your specific team, look around at your company to understand opportunities on other teams where you do more project work and you're not always on call since you work more with local colleagues. How will you find those other teams? Will HR give you that information? Will your manager? Is there an internal online toolkit? It's not likely that any of those is the case.

The easiest way to find these other opportunities at your current employer is to talk to other moms on other teams or in other departments. Be specific with your networking requests and ask the questions. Find out firsthand about managers and team dynamics. If you're making an internal move to another group, you want your expectations to be in line with those of the manager and team.

You have the resources available to you. It's a matter of asking and finding the right people to talk to. If you're not sure who to talk to within a team, start asking around. Those moms with work-life balance often know other moms in the same situation in another department.

Or see what initiatives might be in place that focus on work-life balance and do some research to understand who heads up the initiatives or is highly involved. Those dialed-in individuals, normally women for women's initiatives, will be able to recommend someone for you to talk to.

Another topic to cover during these networking meetings is previous employers. You can understand the teams, departments, and initiatives at competitors or in related industries or fields. You might even find out about different industries. See what's different and what's similar. Ask why your networking partner left and if she or he would consider going back. Talk about what types of work-life balance initiatives previous employers had in place. Take time to find out more about maternity leave policies and practices. Those initiatives and efforts might not be a match for someone else's needs, but they might be exactly what you're looking for.

Networking Online

People you've worked with in the past have moved on and have moved away. They're still part of your network, but you don't have the usual in-person touchpoints with them. How can you maintain those relationships?

What about meeting people online? You're in an online group

and you see comments from someone that seem smart and relatable. You do some digging and find out that the person is working in the industry or at the company that you want to know more about. He lives across the country though, so you can't meet. Or can you?

A friend of yours recommended you talk to someone she knows, but the person lives in another city that is six hours away. Phone seems impersonal. You're likely not going to drive the six hours. Now what?

You read an article by someone at the company you're interested in, which resonated with you and what you're wanting to do. You want to know more, but the author is nowhere near where you live. Do you give up? Or is there another option?

You can have face-to-face meetings when it makes sense. And you can schedule phone calls. What about using technology to have face-to-face online meetings? Grab your cup of coffee or, if it's late enough, grab a glass of wine, and chat. You get to virtually meet and it's more personal than simply talking on the phone.

Sometimes you can reach out to someone on a platform to connect. Better still, reach out to ask them a question or ask to connect virtually in an online meeting. Some of the women I interviewed for this book were mentioned in articles and I reached out to them to ask if they'd be willing to share their story. It works. The worst that can happen is the person says "no" and the best is that you make a new, meaningful connection.

Networking with Parents at Your Child's School

If you drop off or pick up your child from school, how often do you see the same parents? At least at our boys' schools, I see the same parents over and over.

How often do you talk to those other parents? How well do you know them? If you're like most, probably not very well. You say "Hi" and have light conversation in passing. These parents are a potential network though and you're missing out.

You might be thinking that the person is a SAHM or stay-at-home dad (SAHD) and isn't currently working, but you might not know the complete story. Maybe she or he has a flexible schedule or works from home. Even if the SAHMs and SAHDs aren't currently working, most parents worked somewhere before kids. Maybe the parent previously worked in your field and has some insights about roles with more work-life balance. Maybe his or her significant other, sibling, mom, dad, or neighbor does what you want to do or works at the company you're interested in. Or maybe he or she has a unique blog or project going on that you don't know about. How will you know unless you talk to other parents for networking purposes instead of light chatting?

So, how do you make that happen? There are a few easy ways to learn more about your fellow parents.

There are times when I'm volunteering with other moms and occasionally dads and we often talk about our kids and things happening at the school. Use the time as an opportunity to get to know the other parent better. If you're trying to move from chatting to networking, approach the conversation differently. Take a few minutes to talk about kids and related topics and then shift the conversation. Ask that person about work, education, etc., and use those responses as springboards for continued conversation.

What about at kids' parties when you're not simply dropping off kids? At most kids' parties, there is time when you're not totally focused on kids. Even at the parties that my four-year-old attends, it's still not 100 percent focused on kids. I have time to chat with other moms (or dads) and keep an eye on my child. Again, it's natural to talk about your kids in these settings, but why not ask, "What are you working on these days?" That can open the conversation to other non-kid topics and opportunities for networking. Keep in mind that maybe it's not the best idea to talk about work stuff at a child's birthday or maybe it is. You will know which way to go. Maybe it is your chance to schedule something another time. And, if it is a drop-off party, reach out to a mom or dad whose child is going and say you'd love to grab coffee while the kids are at the party.

Not sure how to transition to non-kid topics? Try one of these questions:

- "What do you do when your kids are in school?" If the answer to this is "I work" then the conversation should be easy to transition to non-kid topics after that. If the answer is SAHM or SAHD, then find other questions to help you understand more about life and career before kids.

- "Do you volunteer outside of school?" If so, ask about various aspects of that volunteer organization or the area of focus that the organization covers. That can be an easy segue into talking about life before kids, personal and professional areas of interest, and professional skill sets.

- If something like a holiday is fast approaching, you can ask about holiday plans. If they talk about seeing family, it's a great time to ask about family. How many siblings? Where do they live? What do they do?

The idea is to transition the conversation away from kids and start talking like professional adults, so that you can guide the conversation to how you would when you network, instead of chatting as two parents. And that gets them thinking of you as someone other than a mom at his or her child's school, which is helpful. You never know when parents from your child's school might come across opportunities that might be of interest to you moving forward.

In my case, I have gone from light chats with fellow moms to interviewing moms for my book, making countless professional connections, and even getting the opportunity to do some training. I even got ideas for the book and potential future courses and training based on conversations with other moms where we dove into professional topics and things they felt were necessary or currently missing in the marketplace.

Keep in mind that only you know when the time is right to have the conversations and do the transition. If someone is clearly in a hurry, it's hard to have a real conversation, let alone dive into topics you want as part of a networking interaction. Don't try to have the conversation when you're both hurrying to pick up when minutes matter or when one of you is clearly trying to drop off and get somewhere. You can tell by his or her body language and pace of walking.

If you're both usually in a hurry, consider scheduling a coffee date, happy hour, or even a walk one day (bonus to fit in some exercise while networking). If you choose the walking route, I recommend you take your phone to either record ideas you might get or to take impromptu notes. And let the other mom know what you're doing at the beginning of your walk so that you don't randomly grab your phone and start recording. A simple "I might record a few notes to remember specific points later" will let them know what's going on. Do not record the whole conversation but do jot down notes to remind you of a specific topic or a potential contact. If you want to take lots of notes, don't do a walk and try the coffee date route, where you can take a notebook.

The conversations can be very productive or they can be light.

And look at cues that tell you whether to keep things light versus trying to more of a networking conversation.

Get to Know Your Neighbors Better

How well do you know your neighbors? If the answer is not very well, maybe it's time to get to know them. It can be as simple as taking over a treat, homemade or store bought, and knocking on the door. Mention you're trying to get to know your neighbors and would love for them to come over for the next breakfast treat, afternoon coffee date, or whatever works. Maybe your kids are a similar age and they can play while you chat. You can even ask him or her to take a walk one morning or evening without kids. Or, if both sets of kids are stroller age, take a walk with kids in strollers. It's hard to take pen and paper with you on a walk, but similar to when you exercise with parents from your child's school, you want to be able to take impromptu notes.

Does your neighborhood have a playground or play area where you see parents with their kids? This is a perfect place to meet moms and dads. Start up a conversation and see what they do when they're not at the playground, playing with their child(ren).

In my neighborhood, there are many moms who work from home or have a flexible schedule, so we've chatted on the playground. We often start the conversation by talking about our kids and then shift to more professional topics. You chat with someone while your children play–a win-win.

Social Gatherings

All of us attend social gatherings, such as book club, happy hour with friends, or parties. Have you ever considered that you can network at these events?

If you're in a book club, do the other book club participants know and understand your skill set or know what you might be looking for, if you want a change? These people who you see regularly can be primed and ready as a network if we know each other's skills, areas of interest, and whatever we're looking for. In that same book club, do you know what their significant others do? If not, simply ask. You can even phrase it as "remind me what your significant other does," if you think this topic has been covered in the past. The idea is to get people thinking about you in a professional setting. You never know when that person is talking to a neighbor, sibling, or even past colleagues or clients, and there could be a potential opportunity for the right role or networking contact primed to chat with you.

The last time you went to happy hour with friends, what did you talk about? Maybe you chatted about a challenge some of you are going through with kids or your significant other. Did you complain about your mother or mother-in-law? Those things are important and help you in so many ways on a personal level, so they should be part of the conversation.

However, did you talk about professional stuff you're working on? Did you share a professional (or even personal) win? Something you're proud of that you want to continue in another way? Did you talk about the change you are trying to make professionally? Do your friends know you're looking for more work-life balance? If not, why not? Aren't these the people most likely to recommend you to those they know? Talk to them about what you're looking for. It doesn't have to dominate the conversation, but you can start to plant the seeds about what you want. Ask them for an introduction after you've done your homework about potential connections. You don't want things to be one-sided, so ask what they're working on, and figure out where you might be able to help them.

A huge benefit with happy hour and book club is that you don't have to put as much effort into transitioning the conversation away from kids. These are likely friends or at least acquaintances. They might ask a few things about kids and then it's easy to move on to more adult- and career-focused conversations.

And, what about getting to know the people who you don't know at the happy hour? There is often a tight group and sometimes there are new faces. Get to know new people. And it can be as simple as, "I don't know you yet. I'm _____." Simply start the conversation with the new person. You have something in common because you're both at the birthday party, happy hour, etc.

What about the holiday events you attend for your significant other or a charity you're involved in? It's a social gathering, where you can casually talk about your interests or learn from those around you. Or maybe it is your chance to make a connection and schedule a lunch or coffee. You probably have your phone so you can access your schedule. Make sure it's appropriate though. Maybe it's not the best idea to talk about work stuff or maybe it is. You will know which way to go.

And you never know where these connections pop up. I'm part of a small local women's business group. We share ideas, give each other recommendations on resources, or respond to requests posted to the group page asking for advice. The first year I joined, I went to the holiday gathering at someone's house. I knew two people in the entire room and decided to mingle with others. I met a fellow mompreneur and, several months later, I worked with her on a business challenge she was having. And over the years, we've stayed in touch and met for coffee or lunch. She introduced me to at least four or five moms I interviewed for this book. They were past clients in her coaching business over the years. Would I have found other women to interview? Sure. But she was a great connection to some fabulous interviews and she was willing to open up her network when I shared what I was working on. And it all started because we spoke at a social gathering years ago.

You Know who to Meet with, but How do You get the Most Out of it?

You've got the networking meetings set up, but now what? Here are some ideas on how to prepare for those in-person or online networking opportunities and make the most out of the time and interaction.

Do Your Homework

Regardless of who you're speaking with, do your homework. If you made the connection through a mutual contact, ask him or her for some initial information. If not, there are a lot of places to find information. Research the person's background, which can be done on LinkedIn or even Facebook, where people often list their current and previous employers and areas of interest. Or do a simple online search to see if he or she was mentioned in an article. If the person is involved in an organization, maybe she is also highlighted on their website as a volunteer or activist.

You don't need to write a research paper on the person, but do try to be educated on the initiatives he or she is working on now and has done in the past. These are great topics to bring up during the chat if they pertain to the conversation. They're also great topics to help you understand steps this person took to get to their current level, department, or role.

Know What You Want to Cover

It's great to have natural flow to the conversation, where it organically covers all the topics you might be interested in. It's more likely you'll get the most out of it if you prepare and have an idea of what you want to cover so you can guide the interaction. That way you can have some natural conversation and times where you guide the dialogue.

Maybe you want to talk about his or her current role, but what about it? Are you asking about how he or she got into that role, what he or she does each day, or a combination? Only you know what you want to cover. And, to some level, you can control the flow of the conversation, but you need to make sure you know where you want it to go. It's easy to get sidetracked in conversations with new people.

If it's helpful to create this in a written document, then do that, even if it's bullet points to remind you of specific topics. You can share as the meeting starts that you want to make sure you cover topics X, Y, and Z. When you meet with people, they generally want the conversation to be beneficial because they often don't have time to meet again soon. Maybe they can follow up with an email or two, but their time is generally limited, like yours.

Limit the Time You Talk about Your Kids

Do not *only* talk about kids, especially to fellow parents. As moms, we can talk all day about our kids—how amazing they are, our struggles as parents, and even the fun things we're doing as a family. Cover the topic of kids and family stuff and move on. As much as you might want to talk about a challenge or solve someone else's challenge with something related to kids, that is not the purpose of the conversation.

Guide the Conversation

As the initiator of the conversation, it's your role to manage and guide the conversation. It's important to not abruptly change the conversation, because no one likes to be cut off and you don't want that to set the stage for the conversation. Figure out an easy, natural transition from the topic of kids to other areas. For example, talk about kids for a few minutes, which does require you keep an eye on time. Then, as a transition, ask how the other parent keeps all the balls in the air. Ask about his or her time management or tips and tools for keeping everything on track. It will make the transition to talking about the professional side of things easier. You can figure out what works transition-wise for you and seems natural. And practice, if you need to, so that it's not awkward or forced.

Don't do All the Talking

Are you excited and passionate about the topic you're talking about? That is great, but it might also be a hindrance. You don't want to do all the talking during this conversation. Articulate what you're looking for in a two- to five-minute elevator pitch. Practice your pitch at home or even in the car when you don't have kids with you. You want your pitch to be natural and easily flow off your tongue.

Another point to consider is your communication style. Do you talk a lot? I'm a talker and I know it. In the end, I want to network, not have the other person write my biography. I am aware of how much I talk and you might need to be as well. Make your sharing concise and purposeful.

Alternatively, what happens if you're meeting someone new and you're not very outgoing? You need to show a level of enthusiasm and confidence during your interaction. Again, practice, practice, practice. Make sure you practice aloud and not only in your head. You might see places where you naturally get tripped up as you explain what you've been working on and what you want moving forward.

While networking might seem like a daunting task, it's a chance to get to know people. These new connections might introduce you to a new opportunity. Treat the interaction less as a line item on the to-do list and more as a new person who you connect with. These new people can potentially be in your life for years to come or they might be a gatekeeper to someone amazing. Enjoy it!

Follow Up

This is the part that I think people forget. We use the advice from our networking interactions and we move on. Circle back to the person you have just networked with. Make sure you take care of any next steps as quickly as you can after you meet. If you say you're going to send something to the person who you've been networking with, do it. You might have mentioned an article or a resource you use; email it with any pertinent information. Connect the dots so the person understands how this relates to your recent conversation. For example, "Jane, I mentioned that I use a resource for my research on X topic. Since you're looking into that topic, you might find the tool I use helpful."

If you've met with someone and want to leave an impression, send a note via email or, better yet, a handwritten note (if you know the person's address). It can be a simple thank you for their time or share a tidbit you found incredibly helpful or enlightening from your conversation.

And keep in touch with this person over time, so that if you do reach out again, there won't be a long lag between communications.

You can send articles that relate to his or her business or project, or resources or press releases on something they're involved with. Share information as you find it. Don't send too much though, since that can be a bit overwhelming on the receiving end. You're looking to keep the connection alive over time.

Return the Favor

While some people might network with you and introduce you to others they know as an act of kindness, some may want something in return. Or you might want to offer something, but what? Ask what that person needs. What is he or she working on that you might be able to help with? You might have a skill that is missing on his or her team or maybe you know someone who could be a good resource. If you can't help with a particular topic or area, do you know someone who can? If not, perhaps this isn't the best use of your skills and offer something that still might help solve that challenge. Or ask if you can be helpful in another area, where you can provide some expertise or connections. See if they know someone who needs help with something or an introduction to the industry you work in.

Networking Playdates

I'm including a concept in this chapter that has slightly different parameters, but it's still a networking where you are type of opportunity. Instead of asking another mom you'd like to network with to take time away from her kids or work stuff, how about you both take time *with* kids to network? Pick a fun spot for kids— playground, park, splash pad, whatever works. Somewhere the kids are generally safe and can play together. The kids are entertained and likely having fun with limited effort from moms and moms get to network. Win-win for all participants. It's also great to do during summer and winter breaks when parents are trying to figure out what to do with kids.

The ways to get the most out of it are a bit different than usual networking interactions, so here are some things to consider.

- If your kids are the about same age, great. If not, do your kids play with kids who aren't their own age? Choose a good spot for kids of a variety of ages or skip the networking playdate if your kids won't play with kids who aren't their age.

- You want a location that all the kids find fun without their mom's constant nudging and attention. For example, don't take infants who can barely walk to a playground designed for kindergarteners or that mom will constantly be distracted by her young child's safety.

- Make sure your kids aren't tired or hungry and try to avoid times when this will be the case (e.g., skip afternoon get-togethers if your kids need a nap). You know what works and what doesn't for your children, and make sure you know what works and doesn't for the other kids involved.

- Take care of logistics and know the basics of the location, if you're the one who suggested the location. What time does the place open and/or close? Where are there restrooms? Is the area shaded? If not, bring sunblock for all the kids. Is there going to be loud music playing? Is it fenced in or is it attached to an area where kids can easily get lost or wander off? Do you need to meet in the front if it's large or is there an easy meeting place? You get the idea. As the initiator of the playdate and probably the location as well, know what you're getting into.

- If you are receiving all the benefit for this networking inter-action, pay for whatever your networking partner and her children get or any fees associated with the location. Pay for a drink, treat for the kids, etc. It's a small expense in comparison to what you're getting. Consider it business etiquette.

- If the place you're going doesn't serve food and beverages, take snacks that have widespread appeal for kids, which are acceptable to other moms (e.g., cut up fruit and maybe something like animal crackers that most kids love), and avoid the unusual things your kids love. It seems like anytime kids start playing, one says, "I'm hungry" and they all nod their heads, even when they've *just* eaten. The idea is to take something to give to *all* the kids, not only yours, whenever they do get hungry. Because they will.

- And, finally, enjoy yourself and don't stress too much. You're being productive and your kids are occupied, most likely having fun.

In summary:

Network where you are each day to take advantage of your limited time as a working mom.

- Take advantage of the built-in networks you have around you, both personal and professional.

- Be specific with your networking approach and strategy.

- Do your homework before you meet.

- Know how you want to guide the conversation.

- Make sure you follow up.

- Return the favor whenever you can.
- Limit your time to talk about kids and know how to transition away from kid-related topics.
- Consider networking playdates with other moms.

CHAPTER 8

MENTORS AND SPONSORS

YOU WANT A TRIBE YOU CAN speak with about your situation and challenges. Let's move things further along on the networking spectrum.

When it comes to the professional side of things, it's great to have support from colleagues and those in similar roles. They can be great sounding boards.

What other roles can support you on the career front? It's important for working moms to have both mentors and sponsors as part of their tribe. Each one has a different role in the life of a working mom and they're equally important. And, make no mistake, it's not only about working hard that keeps you moving up in the ranks. You need people in your corner giving you advice on the next step and even advocating on your behalf. You want the right kinds of career advisors in your corner to help you maximize your efforts.

Mentors

Mentors are a great resource when it comes to getting feedback and advice on options, ideas, and overall career path and choices. There are some things that will help you find and keep the right mentor(s).

Before we get into the tips to help you with finding the right mentor(s), I want to suggest two things. First, be strategic in your overall approach to finding a mentor. Find the right people to talk to based on your specific needs.

For example, you want at least one working mom who is more seasoned than you. She has been doing the working mom thing for longer, so she'll have knowledge of maneuvering that you can tap into. She can speak to ups and downs and ways to avoid mistakes in your career and in work-life balance in general. As a bonus, she's likely to have ideas on how to deal with different scenarios your kids are going through. She'll know what things went well and what to avoid as you progress on your career path as a working mom. Another group that you can look into as potential mentors is those more senior people at your employer or in your industry, who are strong advocates of working moms, which includes men and women. They might or might not be parents, but they will have good advice for you as a working mom.

And the second suggestion is to find a few mentors, essentially like your own board of directors. You want different and various perspectives for the diverse opportunities and challenges that come up. Even consider different levels of experience as well as different types of roles, maybe even within the same department. Hint: It might be interesting for your mentors to meet each other as a chance for them to network as well.

In addition to traditional mentors, you can also consider peer mentoring. This is similar to a mastermind of people at around the same level in their careers and journey. Fellow moms might be dealing with challenges you've already dealt with or vice versa. Many of these tips apply for finding peer mentors as well.

- *Take Your Time.* You want to build these relationships over time, instead of trying to force an unnatural relationship. It's helpful to start having conversations before they become necessary. And you want the time to find the right fit without feeling the pressure to simply talk to anyone available. Part of mentorship is finding the right fit for your personality and your needs.

- *Decide what you are looking for.* Understand what you want in a mentor and why. Ask yourself what questions you want a mentor to help you answer. Think through these elements before you even reach out.

- *Set goals.* Be upfront with what you want to achieve with a mentor. Decide what this looks like and how you will measure it, so that you can see if a mentor is meeting your needs (and vice versa).

- *Find a good fit for personality, style, and approach to career.* This is a professional relationship, but you want to make sure there is a good fit personally and professionally. You are asking this person for career advice and want to make sure your personalities and career approaches mesh. It's hard to ask for advice that you can follow if your personalities aren't even in the same spectrum.

- *Don't feel you must mimic his or her path.* You want someone whose advice you can follow, but you don't have to follow the same path. You might not even be looking for a mom or even a woman as your mentor. You can find someone who took a different approach to his or her career, but you want someone to provide strategic and sound advice on career and life opportunities.

Finding the Right Fit

You've found someone that you'd like to call your mentor, but how do you know if it's the right fit for you and your needs?

- *He or she understands your needs and goals.* When you ask questions or look for advice from your mentor, does he or she clearly demonstrate an understanding of what you're looking for? Is the advice actionable in your situation or does it need to be adjusted a lot to be applicable or even usable in your circumstances? If the answers to these questions and the outcome is that his or her insights and advice help you overcome challenges or improve the outcome of your challenges, you have someone who understands your needs and goals, and he or she is likely a keeper.

- *You have a new perspective or deeper understanding after you speak.* You are excited to meet because you're curious to hear his or her thoughts on a new potential opportunity or career challenge. You find clarity to help you with your challenges as a result of interactions with your mentor, which also shows he or she understands your situation.

Establish Communication Approach or Style

You've found someone to be your mentor, so now what? Put a few things in place upfront, so that you can get the most out of the interactions.

- *When?* Decide how often you will meet. You might even put a few preliminary dates down on the calendar upfront since it might be hard to find time on his or her calendar. Be aware of how busy this mentor is before you ask for meetings that might be too frequent.

- *How or where?* Decide how you'll meet. If he or she is in the same city, do you want to meet for coffee or lunch? If coffee, is that first thing in the morning or in the afternoon? What happens if the person travels a lot and isn't in town on the date you picked? There are many virtual options for online face-to-face interactions or simply do a phone call. You have these same virtual options if the person doesn't live in the same city as you. Figure out the logistics upfront, so that questions won't come up later. Include applicable information on the meeting invite (e.g., online meeting login information or physical location).

- *Formal vs. informal.* Figure out the style or vibe of the interactions and overall communication. This will be largely based on your own personality and that of your mentor. See what fits and what is needed based on personality, expectations, and schedules.

Tips to Get the Most Out of Each Interaction

- *Prepare for your interactions.* You want to be respectful of his or her time (and of your own), so ensure you prepare for your meetings, whether in-person or virtual. Do your homework and be prepared with your questions or challenges you want help with. Write things down so that you don't waste time trying to figure out topics to cover. And have notes for your own points that you probably won't share, but they give you more background or remind you why you might want to ask a question or provide context.

- *Consider sending an agenda or at least points you want to cover.* Send something beforehand to your mentor, so he or she knows what you'll be talking about. You especially want to send this if you think your mentor might want to do research or think through a past situation. An agenda is a must if your interactions are more formal.

- *Be engaged during your interaction.* Your mentor is largely there for your benefit. Make sure you use active listening skills. Ask clarifying questions. Be attentive and maintain eye contact. You want to clearly show you're listening and engaged.

- *Be open to constructive criticism.* Your mentor may see things going on that you don't and provide feedback. Listen to those insights and to the constructive criticism. The idea is to learn, so take full advantage of the relationship.

- *Follow up and say thank you.* Make sure that you follow up after the interactions and say thank you to your mentor for his or her time, insights, advice, etc. This is time away from other activities for your mentor, so show your gratitude. A simple email (especially if you're sending a link) is great. (And don't forget a handwritten note as another option.) Talk about what you learned from the interaction. Follow up with anything you said you would provide such as a resource, article, or information on a specific author or expert who your mentor might find helpful.

Give and Take

A mentorship is a two-way street. So, how can you help your mentor? Can you provide a perspective to a challenge he or she has? Figure out what you can help him or her with and do it. You want this to be mutually beneficial. Send an article you find on something he or she talked about. You might hear about an event on a subject he or she is researching. Share what you know about a topic you might know a lot about that he or she is starting to work on. Be generous with your time and knowledge and share what you find.

Evaluate Over Time

Your needs might change over time and that could mean you need a slightly different mix of people giving you career advice. People might have less time to spend helping with your career decisions, or maybe you find someone who is a better fit for your specific needs in a specific moment. Maintain relationships with the men and women who have been your mentors, even if they are no longer in a mentorship role. You never know when your paths may cross again.

Final Tips for Successful Mentorship Relationships

There are a few more tips I suggest you integrate into this relationship that might result in an even better relationship with your mentor.

- *Be flexible.* It might be as simple as changing dates or switching to a virtual meeting to save time on a busy day.

- *Be proactive.* Figure out in which areas you can be proactive and do it. For example, send articles that you come across that you think might be helpful and connect the dots for your mentor instead of simply passing on an article.

Sponsors

Although I didn't realize it at the time, I often had a sponsor at the large marketing agencies where I worked throughout my career. They were often the senior lead on the team who were direct reports of the senior leadership team at the office or company. They saw something in me and were willing to give me access to new opportunities and help position my skills to new potential managers. I considered them mentors, but they were so much more than that. Now I know they were actually more like sponsors.

In larger companies, it's also recommended you seek out sponsors (this might also be helpful in larger small companies). Unlike mentors, sponsors will promote your accomplishments and skills, help you make connections with more senior leaders inside and outside of the company, and help you get more visibility (e.g., recommending you for or engaging you on a new or existing high profile initiative).[1] Essentially, they're more action-oriented than mentors.[2]

When it comes to working moms trying to create more work-life balance and making productivity or time management changes, sponsors can talk to a manager or senior leaders and advocate about the benefits, helping pave the path. Or they can help position you for an existing or new role that allows for more work-life balance.

As an entrepreneur, you might be thinking that sponsors don't apply to you. Here's the thing—they do. Sponsors for entrepreneurs are different than those in a company, but they serve the same kind of purpose. These are people willing to give you access to their own network, but it's more than simple networking.[3] These are people who will open doors and make introductions with a seal of approval.[4] They might give you access to new customers or to investors, if you're looking for funding, who they know and might have done business with.[5] They could even introduce you to potential new members of your team.

Now that you understand more about the role of a sponsor, the question then becomes how to find them.

Look at Your Network

To find a person who acts as a sponsor for you, analyze your current network. See if you have a connection who is currently a mentor at a senior level or was previously a manager or even a manager's manager. They might also be people who have left the company and are still highly respected. These are people who have moved up the ranks. It's helpful to find people who understand your role and haven't been in your shoes too long ago so they can still relate to your situation. The people in this role must be willing to take on a more active role in your career moving forward.

Look for senior people in your current network who have given advice that you have used and can show how their advice made a difference in your career or specific situation. If you've followed their example in your career, that is another element to share with potential sponsors.

Consider Previous Projects

If you've worked on a high-profile project in the past few years, consider reaching out to someone senior who seemed impressed with your work. He or she has already seen you in action and understands what you've done and what you're capable of. These men and women can see how you could help support their legacy at the company.

Create Opportunities to Work with Potential Sponsors

If you have someone in mind who you'd like to work with as a sponsor at your employer, try to create a situation where you can work together to show your skills and make the connection.[6] It can be hard to do at a company or as an entrepreneur, but there are opportunities to step forward and ask to be placed on a project with someone you'd like as a sponsor in the long-term.

Not sure how to make that happen? Find out what projects he or she is starting and see how your skills match up. Take the initiative and reach out to the person. Say you'd like to work on his or her project because you think you can contribute your skills, expertise, and background, and you'd like to learn from him or her.

You can also get to know a potential sponsor outside of the office. This can be hard to achieve, but look at organizations that the potential sponsor volunteers with and find ways to get involved with that organization. It's even better if there are ways to volunteer that highlight your skill set.

What Can You Do for Your Sponsor?

As with any relationship, a relationship with a sponsor should go both ways. They too are looking at people to sponsor and want someone who can help support their long-term impact on a company.[7]

Are there elements to what you do, either within a company or with your own business, that can benefit your sponsor?[8] For example, as an entrepreneur, are you creating a product or service that might be helpful to your sponsor in some way, whether personally or professionally? If you're at a company, can you provide some sort of support, such as giving perspective of the target market that your sponsor is aiming for with a new project? Essentially, can you help your sponsor achieve his or her goals for a new project? Do you have skills that might be helpful for your sponsor (e.g., social media or financial skills)?[9] If you're in doubt, ask how you can help support your sponsor and his or her initiatives.

In summary:

- Outside of colleagues and your manager, there are generally two groups at work who form your support network: mentors and sponsors. Both can be helpful to an entrepreneur or employee who continues to move through the company ranks.

- Mentors provide guidance on your career decisions.

- Sponsors are more action-oriented when it comes to creating opportunities at work.

CHAPTER 9

ENTREPRENEURSHIP AND WORK-LIFE BALANCE

ARE YOU THINKING THAT YOU'RE not going to find the right work-life balance at a company or even in your industry, so maybe it's time to start you own business? Perhaps entrepreneurship will help you with your long-term work-life balance goals. With that in mind I wanted to include a chapter to help you figure out if this is the right answer to what you need. This isn't a chapter on the step-by-step process to start a business, though. There are many resources available to walk you through that available in the marketplace. Take a look at Resources on **www.mompowerment.com** for links to those.

Entrepreneurship Statistics

You've been pondering starting a business. Curious about what entrepreneurship looks like across the United States? Here are the quick facts to consider about small business in the United States, including mompreneur statistics:

Entrepreneurship is vital to the US economy. There are almost twenty-nine million small businesses or about 99.7 percent of US businesses, according to a 2016 report from the Small Business Administration.[1] Those small businesses employ almost fifty-seven million US employees, which translates to about 48 percent of the private sector workforce.[2] To break that down further, "Established businesses with fewer than 50 employees make up almost 68 percent of all employer firms in the United States and are a source of local economic activity."[3]

A report commissioned by American Express OPEN estimates about 38 percent of small businesses in the United States are majority-owned by women, which translates to over eleven million businesses and almost nine million employees.[4] From an economic perspective, women-owned businesses are generating more than $1.6 trillion.[5]

You might be wondering how women-owned entrepreneurs do when they start their businesses. In 2016, First Round Capital, a venture capital firm that invests seed stage money in start-ups, provided lessons learned after ten years in business. The company found that "investments in . . . companies with a female founder performed 63 percent better than [their] investments with all-male founding teams."[6]

Let's talk mom-owned businesses, since this book is all about moms. Of the women-owned businesses out there, it's estimated that one in three is owned by moms.[7] If you do the math, that's more than three million businesses. That number is amazing! Moms are succeeding every day in starting and running their own businesses. It can be done—with a family. Yay mompreneurs!

Consider Some Financial Questions

Questions to Consider as a Potential Entrepreneur

If you're starting a business, there is often a degree of uncertainty, especially at the initial stages. And this can be the case, even with seasoned professionals who have strong networks, as I saw in my interviews. There are benefits to being an entrepreneur though, including a potentially much higher hourly rate. This makes understanding your own situation that much more important. Consider speaking to a tax professional or financial planner to understand the financial implications of your entrepreneurial endeavor.

- What are your expectations for business in the first year? In the first five years? How does this compare to your current salary?

- Have your current clients already agreed to go with you if you start your own company or do you have new clients lined up?

- If your significant other doesn't have access to healthcare through work, what will coverage cost you?

- Consider employment taxes (e.g., social security) as well as short-term and long-term disability.

- If you had life insurance through your employer, how will you get life insurance moving forward? What will it cost?

- Have you considered the tax implications of starting your own business?

- What are the costs to start up your own business in your state or city?

- What expenses will you have for tools and services to do your job?

Drop in Income Level

If you do decide to try to start a business, there is an element of financial inconsistency, especially at the beginning, so make sure to consider the financial implications of your decision. You might have a drop in income level or there might be retirement implications.

How will you deal with that decrease in income? I don't have the answer, but I do have questions to get you started on understanding the implication of a pay cut, even in the short term.

- What changes, if any, will you and your family need to make if your income level falls, however small?

- Will you need to make changes in the types of activities in which your children are involved?

- Are there any services that you might need to rethink (e.g., housekeeper)? Hint: This might seem like an easy line item to remove, but read Chapter 12 before making that change. For example, instead of removing these services altogether, consider reducing the level of service. You could have a cleaning service come every other week or once a month instead of each week.

- What level of income do you need? Hint: Figure out what monthly expenses you need to cover, including things like retirement or 529 savings. Keep in mind that some of your costs, like childcare after school, might go down, so make those adjustments in your budget as well.

- How much do you need to make to not have any lifestyle changes?

- Can you create a passive income stream to continue to have a higher level of income now, which will continue even when your income gets back to its current level?

Retirement

When you decide to start your own business, it's not only the short-term potential decrease in income that you need to consider. Even if your income doesn't go down, there can be long-term implications, including retirement. Start thinking through the impact on retirement to help you understand if this change in your career approach is right for your situation. Especially as an entrepreneur, there is upside to doing well when it comes to retirement. Talk to your current HR department and/or a financial planner to understand further implications as they relate to retirement.

- Are you planning on retiring soon?

- Does your retirement plan require your current income?

- Is your overall retirement plan flexible?

- How close are you to your retirement goals?

- Can you make up any lost income in a few years?

- Can you create something that allows for passive income to make up the difference in retirement funds you might miss out on in the early stages of creating your business?

Benefits of Entrepreneurship According to the Interviews

Maybe you're wondering what you get out of being an entrepreneur. You might be asking why even consider this as your next step or a possibility down the road. There is no doubt that being an entrepreneur can be hard work, especially in the initial stage. There are many benefits though, starting with building the business you want at your own pace. When I looked specifically at benefits from the perspective of mom entrepreneurs who shared their story with me, the number one benefit was time with family and number two was flexibility. More satisfaction with and happiness in their lives, more options, and balance round out the top five benefits. The financial side of things, where you can potentially work less and make more, does make the top ten list from the interviews, and is a major draw for some mompreneurs.

Is Entrepreneurship Right for You?

I have had my own business doing marketing consulting since the summer of 2012. At the time I had been doing my business as a side hustle for about eight years. I enjoy the flexibility and control of my schedule that entrepreneurship has allowed in this stage of motherhood. It's also interesting and hard work at the same time. Entrepreneurship isn't for everyone, though.

The burning question is whether becoming an entrepreneur is right for you. As with other questions I've shared, I can't answer that. I can get you thinking about entrepreneurship in a different way to see if it's the right fit for you.

Almost 40 percent of moms who shared their stories with me started their own business. Some moms know they want to be an entrepreneur, even if it's years away, which was the case for some of the moms I spoke with. It was relatively easy for them to know it was the right next step.

For other moms, their then employer clearly didn't demonstrate an understanding of work-life balance. Many of these moms looked at opportunities outside of their then current employer and still couldn't find what they were looking for, so they created what they wanted. It was the right time and they felt comfortable with their level of experience and depth of knowledge.

Uncertainty and Entrepreneurship

A marketing consultant for consumer packaged goods in Dallas, Texas, shared that the "Risk and the first six months were brutal, in general. I felt pressure and uncertainty because I had no history [as an entrepreneur] initially, even with a lot of experience in corporate America." She's now been an entrepreneur for years and is sought after for her skills and knowledge. She suggested getting your financial ducks in a row before starting your business and being mentally and financially prepared for the potential financial risk.

Can you handle if it takes time from a financial perspective or if there are inconsistencies? Is the risk at a reasonable level or does the financial uncertainty make the overall risk too high? If it does, then entrepreneurship might not be for you.

Let's be honest, not everyone is open to risk. There is the potential for uncertainty for a while when you start a business. You might get clients lined up right away or it may take time. "My biggest challenges are not knowing the future and what my next project will be," shared a consumer packaged goods consultant in the Minneapolis area. Many people are risk averse. If this is you, maybe entrepreneurship isn't for you and that's OK because there are plenty of opportunities at an employer that empowers employees to have more work-life balance.

Business Development and Problem Solving

It's not only about doing work for most entrepreneurs. You are always doing business development, which means you are selling, to some extent, almost all the time as you create a pipeline of potential clients. You might consider someone to do business development, but it's usually once you're much further into your entrepreneurial journey and you have a much more established small business. You can also create affiliate programs to help encourage others to recommend you or refer business to you.

Keep in mind that selling doesn't mean you must be a salesperson, but you do have to be comfortable talking to people online or in person about your business and what you can do for that individual or company. And that requires you to understand the problem you're solving for that individual or company. It's hard to sell anything, even if you're the best salesperson in the world, if you don't understand the problem(s) you're trying to solve for potential clients.

Do You Have a Unique Idea?

You've decided you want to be an entrepreneur, so what is unique about what you're offering, whether a product or service? It might be your skills that make your perspective unique. It might be your experience that sets you apart. Whatever that unique element is, make sure you can articulate it to potential clients.

Do You Have the Right Tools?

Maybe you are thinking you can do what you do for your current employer as your entrepreneurial endeavor. For some, the transition to business owner is relatively easy, especially for industries with a low barrier to entry. Many entrepreneurs have access to all sorts of tools and resources, from low-cost marketing to shared meeting space to technologies that provide big-business tools at small business prices. Technology can help provide lower cost options and make your entrepreneurial journey easier.

What happens if you need specialized tools or resources? For example, if you're a surgeon, you can't simply decide you're going to do surgery on your own without the right resources such as a facility, instruments, staff, insurance, etc. That is an extreme example, but there are tools that you need for your business. You might have access to expensive tools at your employer that make your job easier. Can you get access to these as an entrepreneur without it being cost prohibitive? Is there something similar that is less expensive without impacting the strategic benefit? Think through the resources necessary, including financial ones that you need to start up your business.

Entrepreneurship–The Basics

You've thought through these initial questions and you're thinking that entrepreneurship is a good fit, so now what? Let's talk through the different elements that I recommend you consider as you build your new business.

The initial stage of starting a business will likely take time and effort, according to my own experience and that of the moms who shared their entrepreneurial journeys with me.

My suggestion is to create some sort of business plan. This doesn't have to be 100 pages, but it's helpful to have something to be your strategic blueprint, even if it's basic. This is your guide when you set up your business or need to make new decisions. Check out the Resources tab on www.mompowerment.com for a link to a business plan template.

The Legal Side of Starting a Business

There are many layers to think through when starting a business. One of the places you can start is by considering the legal aspect of your potential new business. How will you set up your business (e.g., sole proprietorship, LLC, or S-Corp)? How you set up your company as a legal entity can impact your business from financials to benefits to liability. There are many online resources about this element or talk to a financial expert or attorney.

Financials of Entrepreneurship

Figure out financial information upfront, including your budget and understanding what you must do for taxes each quarter and year. Talk to an accountant or financial expert and/or look at online resources available to better understand the financial side of things.

A challenge that exists for entrepreneurs, but didn't come up in my interviews, is understanding the financing of your business. Do you need a large sum of money upfront to pay for resources, which includes paying someone to build your website? Do you need to buy online tools? If so, where will the money come from? That financing might come from your own pocket, family and friends, a loan from the bank, or even outside investors.

One of the biggest challenges for entrepreneurs can be inconsistent income. If you have your own business, whether you manufacture something or provide freelance services, you're ultimately relying on others for your income. And that comes with ups and downs financially and maybe even cycles, depending on your product or service. Not all moms are comfortable with inconsistent income. Do what you need to do to either become comfortable with the inconsistency or figure out how to have more consistent income.

Another area that can be harder for women is funding. While this is improving for females, women still don't get their share of investments from traditional resources. Don't forget about non-traditional options, though, where you can crowdsource funds from friends, family, and even reach out to your potential market for the product or service you're providing. Keep in mind that businesses with a female founder historically performed better than all-male teams.[8] If you're looking for investors, regardless of the source, remember that finding initial funding may take time, even with the best business idea.

Define Your Product or Service

I mentioned earlier in this chapter that you need to figure out the problem(s) you're trying to solve. Once you know that, you can start to develop the product or service you're creating. This can be as simple or complex as you need it to be. Use your own knowledge of your industry and potential clients to figure out the right level of complexity.

Consider Your Ideal Client

Ultimately, you want to play to your strength when you develop your niche. You might be saying you want everyone as a client, but I don't recommend this approach. When you try to appeal to everyone, you don't focus on anyone. Build your products and services with a specific niche in mind and go after that specific kind of client. You can become the go-to person for that niche and be incredibly successful.

Focusing on a niche requires you to have deep understanding of that smaller market within the larger marketplace. That includes monitoring if those needs change over time. If so, make changes to the products and/or services you provide. If you can't meet their expectations, they can go elsewhere. If you need to learn new things, take time to attend conferences or take in-person or online courses. Make sure to include this cost in your budget and remember that it's usually an expense you can write off.

Know Your Competitors

You figure out the problem(s) you want to solve and your ideal client and you're set, right? Not quite. You need to understand what your competitors are doing. Do some research online. Understand their approach and their strengths. What can you do to be different and have a unique perspective, product, or service that clients come to you to get instead of going to the competition.

For those considering a field that doesn't have a lot of competition, look at the substitutes that potential clients use. For example, you might want to start an online magazine and you think there isn't any other online magazine in that space, so you're in a good spot. Before you get too excited though look at what is in print in the same category. Understand where else your ideal potential client goes for information. What podcasts are potential clients listening to? Is there an annual conference that provides all the information? Are there key bloggers in the industry that attract your same audience? Substitutes are as important as competitors for many industries.

Marketing

How will you sell your product or service? Develop a plan to get the word out and attract your ideal client. It can be simple and doesn't require deep pockets. Or you can have a multifaceted marketing plan with a substantial budget. Figure out what will work for your business and niche, and be realistic with what you can spend to make things come together.

Pricing

What is your ideal client willing to pay for your product or service? If you're not sure, ask people within your ideal client profile. Develop relationships with your ideal clients through online groups or through mutual connections. Or they may be people in your network already. Talk about your product or service and get their input. See if additional elements you plan on including to add value actually matter. Understand their budgets before you start pricing your product. While your competitors might be a likely place to go to understand pricing, you might be putting out a different level of product (e.g., more value-based or a premium version), so that pricing might give you some ideas or it might not be helpful at all.

Being a Successful Entrepreneur

Create Structure

Life as an entrepreneur is easier if you're organized on the professional and personal sides. Moms talked about organization and creating structure as it relates to their workspace, calendar, and time management. They recommended keeping things consistent and easy to find. It saves time and effort if it's all organized. Plus, at least in my case, it's also less distracting. I have a hard time working at home when things are all over the place.

As an entrepreneur, you likely have flexibility on where you work if you're not heading into an office every day. Figure out your rhythms and plan accordingly. Should you work from home? Do you need to spend time in a coffee shop away from home because your young kids are at home with a nanny? Do you want to rent a desk or spend time in a co-working space? Is it a combination of being at home and away from home that will work best? Figure out how you can be most productive and make it happen.

Create the Right Schedule

Understanding how your time is best used can be incredibly important for your short- and long-term success as an entrepreneur.

Think through how you work best and schedule your time with that in mind. Understanding how you work–your natural rhythm–and even where you work best can make a difference in your productivity and overall abilities. Make sure that your work hours help you be most efficient.

As you build a business, it can be long and hard work. Consider your needs and those of your family, and include them in your schedule. You might think about the long-term time with family, but don't miss out on the short-term in the process. Find the right tools or team members to help with things like project management, which can help with organizing your schedule and timelines.

If entrepreneurship is something you'd like to take a stab at, I will share this final thought specifically about starting a business. A mom who owns her own advertising and sales company in Austin, Texas, shares these encouraging words: "Take control of your destiny because you can make your own path, especially as an entrepreneur."

In summary:

There are various aspects to creating a new business as an entrepreneur.

- Decide if entrepreneurship is something you're interested in.
- Understand the financial side of starting a business.
- Finding your niche in the marketplace can help you be successful in your business.
- Figure out your ideal client and understand how to market to that audience.
- Take time to get organized, which can be helpful for entrepre-

neurs, especially mompreneurs.

- Understand and implement the logistics necessary to set yourself up the right way.

PART IV

SKILLS, TOOLS, AND SYSTEMS THAT HELP YOU GET TO BETTER WORK-LIFE BALANCE

CASE STUDY: Putting Boundaries in Place to Create More Work-life Balance

After working full time for about four years, this health communications professional returned to graduate school for a two-year program. Since then, she has switched back and forth between full-time and part-time roles, based on her family's needs, especially with the birth of her two children. She even left the corporate world for several years, although she always worked—in her family's business and/or as a consultant. She also took advantage of the time away from a consistent schedule to get certified as a yoga instructor and do meditation training.

When her daughter was about two and a half, she started in her current role of doing communications for a department in a major hospital in the northeast and has been there for several years. And she continues to do consulting as a health communications specialist.

This communications professional used her negotiation skills to get the type of role and schedule she wanted. The role was originally full time, but it was new, so the department wasn't sure how much time was really needed to fulfill its needs. She negotiated a reduced schedule, including working half-days on Friday from home. And she shared an interest in expanding the role a bit over time to include other areas of interest for the department, which has since happened. She is able to have the flexibility and time with her family while having a fulfilling career.

Her advice for moms looking for more work-life balance:

- *Work the time you're paid.* If you get paid to work thirty-two hours, then work thirty-two hours. Realize how much time you're working in general, even in a full-time role. Understand how you can be more efficient and effective with your time so that you're not working a bunch of hours for which you're not compensated.

- *Sprinkle in an area of interest from beginning.* As you start a new role, look at what you're interested in that is not included in the job description. Start to share those areas of interest so that you can expand your role over time or even transition into a role that might become available over time.

- *Define boundaries and set expectations early on.* You want to avoid being on call. Don't check email once home with kids or before bed. Often people understand when you're a mom with small children, but you must let them know your boundaries.

- *Figure out your personal boundaries.* You need to know what you need on a personal level as well. Consider the boundaries you put in place with your family and friends so that you maintain your balance and are able to fulfill your own needs.

- *Quid pro quo time at home.* She and her husband have this so that they essentially keep track of time where they have time to themselves (e.g., he got four hours with his buddies for golf, so she gets four hours to do whatever she wants without kids).

CHAPTER 10

PRODUCTIVITY, TIME MANAGEMENT, AND STAYING ON TASK

THE CONCEPTS OF PRODUCTIVITY, time management, and staying on task are closely related. Productivity is making the most of your time. Time management is planning and controlling the time you have. Once you set aside the time and start working, you need to stay on task. For example, I have many things to accomplish in one day. I've set aside two hours to get three blog posts done. Each one will take thirty minutes plus ten minutes to revise, if I'm being efficient with my time. To actually make the most of my time, I must stay on task, which means no social media or checking email. I need all three—productivity, time management, and staying on task—to get those three blog posts written, revised, and ready to go.

Productivity

Those of you who watched my talk from TEDxSMU Women know that productivity is one of my hot buttons. I think there are flaws in how companies look at productivity or maybe I should describe it as there is a lack of measuring employees based on productivity.

The current eight-hour workday commonly used in the United States today was put in place by two large printing firms in 1906.[1] And a federal law, the Adamson Act, was passed by Congress in 1916 to create an eight-hour workday for railroad workers.[2] Today's standard forty-hour work week is commonly linked back to Henry Ford since he instituted this schedule in his factories in 1926 and helped popularize this approach.[3]

It's almost 100 years later and we make and do all sorts of new things, but we still use that forty-hour work week as the standard for how we measure people, not their productivity. Essentially, we measure people on hours–at least forty for most salaried employees. Why do we treat all employees the same each day, measuring the number of hours they have worked? And how is it that productivity doesn't play into the daily measurement?

A World Economic Forum study show that employees stop being productive at about twenty-five hours per week.[4] People in roles that require a lot of brain power might have even less productive time.[5]

The other time is unproductive, but employees are still at the office. If you work for someone else, you know what I mean when I say the way you're usually measured is hours working. For things like promotions or bonuses, maybe productivity and contribution come into play. Why isn't productivity used for measuring employees daily? We could reward employees for being more productive instead of requiring them to work for eight or more hours each day.

If you're an employee, you might be thinking, "My manager measures employees by their productivity." Think about it this way. Do you get rewarded for being productive by getting more work, especially to cover someone else who is less productive? Or can you leave early? Chances are, you get more work.

If your employer doesn't look at productivity, they're the norm.

Things have changed since that forty-hour work week was put in place, so maybe it's time to start thinking differently so that we keep great employees engaged. Maybe we need to reflect employees' level of productivity and efficiency, not only hours at work. We shouldn't keep people at the office (or simply working if they work from home) because they have to complete at least eight hours of work each day, without question. We can reward employees for finishing their tasks in fewer than eight hours when they're proven they can reach their daily, weekly, or monthly goals and maintain their standard of work.

Change your Productivity

You want more work-life balance? Maybe you need to change how you work. These are a few approaches that were mentioned in interviews or that I use, but there are many others out there.

It's helpful to understand how you're most productive, so I highly recommend doing some research and trying a few options out to see what works best for you. There are all sorts of ways to be more efficient with your time once you know what you're spending time on.

Figure Out Your Productivity Rhythms

Each person is unique in his or her productivity. Figure out your most productive time, since you're at your peak performance then. Understand your least productive times and consider limiting the amount of work you do at that point of your day or change the types of work you do during your low productivity times (e.g., time to meet as a group, return calls, or respond to email). Seems simple, but it takes you understanding your own rhythms and then using that knowledge to help you with your time management and productivity.

It happens I am at my most productive in the morning and for a few hours in the evening. Early afternoon is when I have my natural lull. I set up my calendar with these elements in mind. For example, I work as much as possible in the morning when I'm at my best. I volunteer mid-day or in the afternoon at our boys' schools or I will schedule non-essential calls (e.g., calls that aren't client-related or don't have direct impact on my business). The idea is early to mid-afternoon isn't active work time.

See what works in your situation and don't be afraid to experiment. It might take a few tries to figure out your best time to work or maybe the best time to work on different elements of your job or to-do list (e.g., writing in the morning versus calls after lunch).

Work on Top Priorities First

It feels good to cross a bunch of things off your to do list throughout the day. If you take that approach, will you spend enough time on your most important tasks? Laura Vanderkam, an expert on time management and productivity and author of *I Know How She Does It* and *What the Most Successful People Do Before Breakfast*, suggests that instead of checking off a bunch of things first, focus initially on priorities and then sprinkle in the rest.[6]

I do major client work and writing as soon as I get back from dropping off my boys at school. Even though it feels good to check a bunch of boxes, it's best to be at my freshest for my priorities, instead of working on my sometimes incredibly long to-do list. In fact, I use a power hour, another suggestion from Vanderkam. I don't check email or social media. I don't generally schedule calls or have meetings, so that I can dedicate the first hour of my day–my most productive time–to strategic, challenging work. It's when I do my best work, so it makes sense, right?

What are you doing during your most productive time? Are you in a standing meeting? Are you on a call with a client to go over a project's status? What can you do to take back that productive time and use it and shift the other calls, meetings, etc. to another time when you're not at your most productive? If you need to be at your best during that meeting or call, by all means schedule it during your power hour, but take back control of that time if that is not the case.

Batching or Time Blocking

At the office, you need both time to work to get things done and time to engage with your clients and team. Boundaries help you divide up that time effectively. Essentially, you establish blocks of time to do different types of tasks. This can also be referred to as batching.

Several moms mentioned batching, which is how I work as well. It's the idea that combining similar tasks makes you more efficient than trying to switch back and forth between different kinds of tasks. When it's writing time, I write several blog posts, guest blog posts, etc. in one block of time or I research for different projects in one block since I'm already in that mode.

I sometimes combine blocks of time with the Pomodoro technique, where I work twenty-five minutes and then do something else for five minutes, and then work twenty-five minutes and do something else for five minutes, and so on. After several of these intervals, I take a longer break.[7]

Use a timer or your calendar reminders. I find it's better to use a timer you must get up to turn off or you'll likely keep working.

Be productive with those five-minute windows as well. Need to post on social media? Do it during those five-minute windows. Need to leave a voicemail when you know someone isn't around or won't answer? Do it during that five-minute window. You get the idea. You don't want to waste the downtime because you'd be shocked how much you can get done in the fringes of your time. And little pockets of time matter when you're trying to find more work-life balance.

Time Management

Tracking Time

Part of being more efficient with your time is understanding how you're spending your time. Vanderkam suggests having a better understanding of how you spend your time over the course of a week: "If you want to lose weight, you keep a food diary. If you want to get out of debt, you record your spending. Likewise, if you want to use your time better, you should keep track of your time."[8]

This is a helpful first step in understanding where your time currently goes before trying to figure out where it *can* go. And it allows you to understand how much time you're using for your various tasks, whether on the professional or personal side. Once you track this and get a good idea of your normal schedule (e.g., don't track during the weekend or holidays), you can start assessing your schedule and what areas you might want to change.[9]

Work during Naptime

An astrophysicist researcher at a university in Austin, Texas, shared that when her kids were young, she made sure to work during naptime. She described it as the naptime hustle. For moms who work from home with young children, this is can be an integral element of time management.

It's helpful to have a plan for what you can get done during naptime. Prepare for it, so that you can be most efficient and productive during the time. Have your prioritized list ready. When our boys were younger, I used the time to work. In addition, I didn't usually schedule phone calls during naptime when our younger son was an infant in case he didn't nap or took the power naps he was notorious for. When he napped for an extra hour, I'd get that much more done from my prioritized list.

If you have a newborn or young infant, consider planning for naptime differently since sleep times can be inconsistent initially. Use small increments of time to be productive. Business expert Dana Malstaff suggests breaking the day down into ten- or fifteen-minute increments and looks at what she can do from her phone, such as read a relevant article or respond to an email from a team member or client. The little pockets of time can keep you, your team, and your clients moving toward bigger goals.[10]

If you notice that naptime is longer over several days, then you can check off more tasks on your to do list. As the naps get longer, break things down into larger chunks and tackle those bigger projects. Always remember to have your smaller goals prioritized, so you can get to it as soon as the clock (so to speak) starts.[11]

Focus

The third part of this trio is the ability to stay on task or focus. It's incredibly important, and time management and productivity don't happen without focus.

Have Specific Goals for the Day

We all have our goals for our projects, but what about your daily goals? To be more efficient on a daily basis, I started creating daily goals so that I know exactly what I have to do each day to build up to my bigger goals. I try to have three to five things that I'm trying to achieve for the day. This requires me breaking down a bigger goal into bite-sized chunks. Some of these things might be something small like registering my child for a school activity, but there is a deadline and a benefit to taking a bit of time to get it done. For work, I might specifically spend one hour researching a specific slice of a topic for a client project. This approach of three to five smaller goals keeps me on task.

If you want to try to break down your goals, you might assign a time period to go along with working on each goal. An event planner and business coach in Chicago suggests "scheduling out your work day in whatever increments [make sense] for you." Her suggestions were fifteen- and thirty-minute segments. And you can align those increments with your goals, so you prioritize. This might help with keeping you on track instead of getting sidetracked by things like social media.

Meal Preparation

Productivity isn't only for your professional tasks. You can improve productivity with your parental or household duties as well. One of the areas most mentioned by moms from their personal lives in interviews was meal preparation. For most of the moms I interviewed, they are the person in charge of household duties on top of being the default parent, which means having dinner on the table falls squarely on their shoulder. There were a few moms who shared they don't cook and that is a responsibility of their significant other, but these were few. (You might remember from earlier that my husband has taken on more of this to lighten my load. If your significant other does the cooking—and does a good job—you have found a keeper, ladies!)

I will also add that this is one of those areas where you can engage help. Can your significant other help with planning the weekly menu, writing out your grocery list, doing the shopping over the weekend, and/or actually do the meal prep? If you have older kids–tweens or teens or even elementary aged kids–they can help with meal prep stuff. It can be a teaching opportunity. Understand where you can empower others to help you.

This is one of those areas where you can get outside help or even look to your tribe to help you. Could you figure out how to do meal prep and help each other? Maybe each batch your meal prep so that you can share meals with your tribe and they do the same? There are even companies that come to your house to prepare several meals for your family. See what options you might have instead of you doing all the meal preparation and planning if you're looking for help in this area.

How can you make meal prep easier? Moms I interviewed shared their tips and I also include my own:

Be More Efficient with Your Time during Meal Prep

- Use a slow cooker, especially on nights when there are evening activities.

- Cook all or most meals on the weekend and freeze whatever won't be eaten in the next two to three days, and then thaw out meals for the end of the week.

- Make enough food for two meals, so that you're only actively cooking two or three nights a week.

- If your family doesn't like having the same meal two nights in a row, have enough entrée for two nights and change the sides (e.g., rice and zucchini one night, and butter noodles and peas another). It takes less time to make the sides than to make two totally different main courses.

- Freeze a meal for another night. We often make enough for three nights. Two consecutive nights we change the sides and we freeze the final portion for another night, when we're under a time crunch.

- Hint: Take time to look at labels to find healthy frozen options you don't mind having in a pinch. Don't feel guilty when unhealthy options fall into your mix from time to time. It's OK. You're doing great and your kids are fine.

Apply Planning to the Meal Prep Process

- Plan meals for the week so that you visit the grocery store only once each week for all ingredients and replace staple items.

- Using consistent themes each day or two days of the week (e.g., taco day(s) versus rice bowl day(s)). Hint: Use the same entrée for two different themes. For example, chicken tacos one day and chicken and rice bowl the next.

- Consider an online service that either delivers groceries on your list or that sends all the ingredients portioned out, so that all you have to do is prepare it. For some meals the prep and cook time is less than 30 minutes.

- Almost every major grocery chain will shop for you for a small fee. Have staples that you usually buy? Order them online and have them ready at the store. And some places will even bring your order out to your car, so you don't have to run in with your kids. That is a huge win if you have young kids. Want to choose some of your own stuff? You can even run in to grab fruits and vegetables or meat, but in a fraction of the time it usually takes for a visit to the store with kids in tow.

Meal Prep Shortcuts

- Making breakfast for dinner is something we do about once every few weeks. It can be pancakes, eggs, oatmeal, or whatever is easy to make that your family loves.

- Wash fruit and veggies and even chop whatever needs to be chopped when it first comes home from the grocery store. It can save time later.

- Wash all the fruits and vegetables for the day in the morning if you're prepping lunches for school. You can even chop up veggies when you're in the food prep zone.

- Figure out how kids can help. I know you're thinking this might take more time, but hear me out. Even young kids can tear lettuce for a salad. My young boys prep what we call cheater guacamole where they scoop out and smash the avocadoes. I pour in bottled salsa and they mix it all up. Are there small tasks that help you in some way? They also feel a sense of accomplishment when they help. It might also get your picky eater to eat more and different things if he or she helped prep them.

Prepping the Night Before

A tip that I heard in many interviews also happens to be something I do as well. Make sure you use the night before to help with your overall productivity.

Work Preparation

When it comes to work, on the night before look at what you want to do the following day, especially in the morning. Set up the three to five goals and decide the most important things on your list. Do anything that might be able to help you get your results the next day. For example, look strategically at how your day naturally maps out with projects, calls, meetings, etc. and plan your day. Put bullet points together for something you're writing. Organize any research you've done so that you can hit the ground running with the project instead of wading through the research first.

If you're heading to a meeting, print out anything you need to physically take and have copies ready. Or put the presentation in a folder you can easily find on your PC desktop or on a USB drive, or email it to yourself. You never know what the morning might look like, especially with kids. All that time you thought you might have in the morning might be spent cleaning up a massive spill or a blowout. You might have to change your black slacks because your sweet toddler hugged you when his hands were covered in cream cheese from his toasted bagel. Or technology might not work, because it seems like that's what happens when you need technology to be your friend. I know you've experienced the moments I'm talking about if you're a working mom. Take care of it the night before and avoid stress in the morning.

Getting Bags Ready

There are personal things you can do at night to help you get your morning going faster. Put your laptop and/or notebooks in your work bag. Get backpacks and baby bags ready with things like labeled diapers and snacks that don't require refrigeration. Make sure you label anything that needs to be labeled (e.g., diapers and food containers), so that you don't have to do that in the morning. (You can get a link to the specific labels I use for everything from water bottles to clothing on **www.mompowerment.com** under the Resources tab.) Once the bags are ready to go the evening before, put them by the door.

Put Things in a Consistent Spot

Our car keys hang on a special hook by the front door. The boys' shoes are always in the mudroom. I don't have time to look for keys or shoes every morning for ten minutes. Have a place for everything, especially the things you use daily. It simply makes them easier to find, so that takes less effort.

Have things ready for the next step. For example, put out lunch boxes with containers on the counter, so you know exactly where they are and won't have to go find them. I put a fun napkin in our boys' lunchboxes, ready to go. It's a small touch that our boys love and it's easy, especially when I do it the night before.

Lunch Preparation

If you're still making lunch for your kids, which is my situation, think about what you can prepare the night before. A few moms I interviewed suggested making the entire lunch the night before. I don't make sandwiches the night before, but I do some prep such as washing fruit or putting things that don't need refrigeration in the lunchbox. I'm also consistent with what I call my "formula" for the boys' lunch. It generally consists of a sandwich, three to four fruit servings, and some sort of treat. Putting the treat into the lunch the night before takes care of one step and also keeps me from forgetting it. We put snacks in the boys' backpacks before we head up for bed as well. Our boys choose and label their snack. The bonus is they feel more empowered when they do this.

Is this an area where your kids can be more independent? I interviewed moms whose kids had made their own lunches starting at age seven or eight. How can your significant other help? Remember, you don't have to be the one who does everything in the morning.

Clothing Choices

Have everyone in the house pick out clothes and lay them out the night before. Both of our young boys now have opinions on what they wear, so it's their choice. I provide input if necessary (e.g., it's picture day or it's going to be 100 degrees, so no long sleeve shirts). It also limits the number of challenges or discussions in the morning and can decrease tears.

A therapist in Alabama schedules what she'll wear for the month, so that she uses no mental energy on this aspect of her life. If you know your schedule weeks in advance or even for the week, you can use this approach to plan your wardrobe for long periods instead of daily.

I have friends who have essentially the same general outfit, but an element changes. They have the same tops, bottoms, and accessories in different colors. It's consistent and requires little mental energy to figure things out, especially if all the items generally color coordinate. You know it will look good on you and you know it all goes together, so it's a low-stress wardrobe.

You might even consider a capsule wardrobe where everything is based on a specific color scheme and style. You know that everything goes together. You can use accessories to mix things up or provide pops of color. It can definitely limit the amount of mental energy that goes into figuring out your wardrobe each day or for each meeting.

To-Do List versus Did List

Anyone who knows me well, knows I love my to-do lists. I keep a single list of everything that needs to be done in both professional and personal areas. My thought is that I'm the one doing it all, so I keep everything on one list broken out into different categories.

What most people don't know is I also have a "did" list, which I highly recommend. In my case, it's the same list as my to-do list. I use my notebook for my to-do list, so my did list is what's been checked off. It helps me see what I've accomplished in a day or week. And that is something that keeps me motivated. Sometimes, you need to see how far you've come on project or see your productive moments. If you do online to-do lists, you can mark through lists as well instead of deleting a completed task. Once you're ready for a new list, keep a separate place to track accomplishments you want to highlight over time.

Adjust as Necessary

Give yourself time and the permission to adjust so that you hit your productivity stride. Some things might work right away and others might take time and small tweaks to get things right.

If you've made agreements with your manager, team, or senior leadership, let them know if you need to make changes if something is clearly not working. Otherwise, give yourself some time and space to make small adjustments in how you're working.

The Importance of Breathing Space

What is breathing space? For me, it's a pause that I take in my day. I might use it to assess the moment and figure out next steps. I take breathing space to confront and combat the feeling of overwhelm when my to-do list seems to be as long as my arm and only getting longer. That pause can really help me think through challenges or come up with that one thing that I can do to get things back under control.

We're all busy. Our lives pull us in all different directions every day. Some days we have it together and some days we barely hold on. We go from one thing to another to keep all the plates spinning at the same time.

Moms describe taking calls in the car while waiting in the pick-up line in efforts to use every hour of the day and be incredibly productive. I am a proponent of being your most efficient and productive when you work. When we do that though, we don't get a moment of transition and we lose the breathing space we might need. We go from professional to mom with no buffer between the two. I try not to do this every school day.

Sometimes I might take an extra few minutes before grabbing my younger son so that I can pause, catch my breath, and shift to the perspective of mom from career woman. I might do a quick guided meditation or one where I let my monkey mind wander and then focus for a few moments. I might listen to classical music or jam out to something that will give me energy. On some days I will listen to an audio book or one of my favorite podcasts. I want to be present in those first few minutes of my interaction with my boys. Even though my husband's commute is only fifteen to twenty minutes, that still allows him to have a transition time from professional to dad and husband.

Include time in your day and week, as an element of your productivity, to assess and address your needs. Maybe intentionally having more breathing space can help with having more have-it-together moments and fewer barely-holding-on times.

Consider the visual version of this concept. In design, the visual aspect is as much the stuff you want to look at as it is the white space around that stuff. You need the two to be balanced or your eye doesn't know where to look. It's too busy and is a sensory overload without focus.

It's the same idea with the breathing space–the downtime–that your brain needs to make the rest of the time more productive and efficient. We simply can't be at our highest productivity 100 percent of the time, even though we might think we can. And, realize it might be different for each person. Some moms use exercise to help them take a pause in their day. Other moms might meditate. Other moms still might practice self-care.

In my case, without breathing space, the *Mompowerment* books probably wouldn't exist. I wouldn't have thought about bringing the stories together in a book, creating a community, and empowering moms to think differently about their own work-life balance challenges.

In summary:

We need to consider how productivity, time management, and staying on task work together.

- Productivity is incredibly important to working moms.
- Track your time to understand how it is spent.
- Understand your natural productivity rhythm and choose which approach to productivity allows you to be most efficient and effective with your time.
- Set goals for the day to get the most out of the day.
- Try to focus on the most important goals or tasks of the day instead of checking off many items from your to-do list.

- Consider dividing up your day into blocks of time instead of responding to requests and tasks as they come to you.

- Prepare the night before to make the following day even more productive.

- Have some flexibility to adjust what's not working.

- Consider adding breathing space in your day to be at your most productive level.

TIPS FOR EFFICIENT MEAL PREPARATION

Use Tools
Consider a slow cooker or insta-pot to cook everything at once.

Outsource
Save time and shop online for pickup or delivery.

Use Weekends
Prep meat and veggies Sunday for the week.

Batching
Save time and cook multiple meals at one time.

Double Up
Double your recipe and freeze half to reheat on a busy day.

Meal Plan
Plan for the week and visit the grocery store only once.

CHAPTER 11

SETTING BOUNDARIES

WE'VE COVERED PRODUCTIVITY, time management, and maintaining focus, but it's hard to do those things if you don't have a structure for your schedule in place. You want a schedule that helps you be at your most efficient and effective. And, boundaries are the cherry on top to keep you on task and make your valuable time even more productive.

Being Strategic with Your Schedule

Being intentional with your time is incredibly important to working moms. You're trying to manage a lot and fit it all in. What does this look like in a day or over the course of a week?

You want to structure your time, whichever approach you choose, so that you're at your best. Katie Krimitsos, founder of the Biz Women Rock community and podcast, shares a great way to look at this. She says that "Your values show up on your calendar." So, what does your calendar or your schedule look like? How are you reflecting your values and what you really want to achieve on your calendar?[1]

Boundaries at Work and at Home

You have a deadline in the next few hours and you have had countless interruptions in person, online, and via phone. Everyone knows that this is an important project and you need to get these final pieces done. Your team, manager, and your clients need to give you some space to finish.

You head home for the day to have dinner with your family or maybe you're at a friend's birthday happy hour. You left the office less than an hour ago and you've received several emails, calls, or texts from your team and client asking for an immediate response. Is it an emergency that needs your attention now or can it wait until you're in the office in the morning? Can't your team figure this out without you? Why can't they respect your time?

What is missing in these scenarios? There aren't boundaries. A consistent piece of advice from about 15 percent of the working moms who I interviewed was about the need to set and maintain boundaries on the professional and personal sides.

The Boundaries at Work are Important at Home

The boundaries that you put in place at work make a huge impact on your time away from the office, especially when you're a mom and trying to spend time with your family. You want to be present with your family. If you're focused on work, especially with interruptions from your colleagues or clients, it's hard to give your family your full attention.

Be Present

When you're at home, are you thinking about work or is work outright interrupting your family time? When you're at work, do thoughts of home and family seep into your day? If you're focused on work stuff at home, you're not enjoying your time with family and friends. Chances are that if you're thinking about or being interrupted by things from home, you're not being as efficient as you can and you're also more likely to make mistakes when you're distracted at work.

It's important to be *present*, whether at work or at home. Figure out the infrastructure you need for home and work to make sure the other side doesn't creep into your day. There will always be emergencies, which are unavoidable, but you can make the non-emergencies stop interrupting your work or personal time.

An Austin-based OB-GYN talked about the ability to be present because of more balance in her life. She said, "It's balance dynamics. When I'm at work, I can focus 100 percent of my efforts on patients; when at home, I can focus 100 percent on my family and partner." The concept of being more present seemed a consistent theme with many moms I interviewed.

For many moms I spoke with, that ability to be present enabled them to lose the mommy guilt. Since they could focus on family when they were with family, they didn't feel like work got the best of them. When they were at work, they could focus on work, knowing that they would spend time with family in a few shorts hours or for an extended period over the weekend.

Boundaries Can Lower Stress

Have you ever considered what stress does to you? It turns out that chronic stress, like from work or other pressures, is bad for your body. It can affect everything from digestion to sleep to the body's ability to fight infection. Your memory can start to suffer. Chronic stress affects your decision-making abilities too.[2]

Time away from the office each day helps manage stress in the short- and long-term. If you can't ever step away from work, stress levels will only go up, which is bad for us. Time away from work lets us decompress and destress. These daily or weekly moments are part of the boundaries you establish to maintain work-life balance. In addition to these small windows of time where you lower stress, consider longer stretches away from work for vacation, regardless of whether you travel somewhere or have a staycation.[3]

Time Away Enables Better Performance

Not convinced of the importance of time away? Let's talk about how time away improves your performance. You need a break each day to recharge and to perform your best. We aren't machines. We can't be productive 24/7. Our brains need to step away from work so that we're at our best.

Think about the number of times you have been working on a project for hours, days, or even months. You stop catching mistakes when you're too close to the project for extended periods of time. If you put down the project for a few hours or days, you start catching mistakes again.

That break at the end of your work day or on the weekend lets you look at your work with a fresh perspective when you start working again. In addition, it's hard to see another viewpoint or find the holes in your own perspective if you can't put something down for a period.

As an additional benefit, interacting with your family and friends might even trigger new ideas. I can't tell you the number of times I've been chatting with my husband at the end of the day or playing with my boys and suddenly a new idea or solution to something I've been working on pops into my head. I'm not consciously thinking about work and my brain has time to process in its own time. (That's also why I almost always have a notebook nearby.) I worked with countless creative people in the past who talked about getting ideas in the shower or on a run. Let your mind think through something passively, while you focus on something else and it might help you as well.

Boundaries Can Help Workflow during Work Time

Boundaries also matter for getting your work done during work time. Put blocks on your calendar for different activities to be more productive with your time. Designate meeting times (some moms had designated meeting days) and work time on your calendar. You don't want your schedule to be so full of meetings that you don't have time to work, so that you must take work home to get it done after a full day of meetings. Sure, this can happen from time to time, but it doesn't need to be your everyday norm. Make sure your manager or senior leadership, team, and clients know about these blocks to manage their expectations and coordinate their schedules.

Consider Personal Boundaries during Work Time

We are always moms, even when we go to work. We don't get to stop being a mom during our important meetings or before a deadline. But we need to separate personal time from work. Establish what a personal emergency is. If you and your spouse both work, which is the norm these days, make sure you have a plan, whether it's day by day or weekly, on who should pick up a sick child or take a sick child to the doctor.

A financial planner in Austin, Texas, and her husband decide who will pick up a sick child and deal with any doctor appointments based on who must cancel fewer meetings during the day. In this scenario, this can be a great option when it's hard for one parent to be the daily default parent.

It's important to consider this because situations come up all the time: a sick child or the nanny calls in sick, so you have to scramble for childcare. Having this discussion upfront or on whatever basis makes sense is essential to maximizing your family's time, not just one parent's. (And consider back-up childcare as an option as well. See more in Chapter 4.)

Implementing Boundaries

The easiest option is to establish boundaries from the beginning of a relationship, whether that is with a new job or a new client. Lay these out upfront and make sure everyone agrees to the work and personal time boundaries. Establish definitions for things like emergencies or when it's appropriate for interruptions.

An event and wedding planner and transformational coach in the Chicago area shared that she sets rules and parameters from the beginning of a relationship with a client. In addition, she suggests setting a clear and concise schedule and building infrastructure around it from the beginning. For her, this includes areas such as a response time of twenty-four hours for email and phone calls. This avoids unrealistic expectations from clients and her team. This mom has set the boundary of not being available for client needs in the evening, unless there is an event she is managing. She is a single mom to four and wants to be present with her kids when they're all at home.

If it's an existing relationship, you might be able to put in the boundaries right away, but chances are you will need to have a period to give time for people to readjust to new boundaries and new expectations. You might need to retrain your clients, manager or senior leadership, or team when you redefine your boundaries. An option is to create a transition plan for yourself so that it's not like a light switch between two sets of boundaries. You can share the transition plan, if that makes sense, or gradually start to lengthen the response time. If you do present a plan, make sure to speak to what is changing (e.g., schedule, hours, response times to voicemail or email). You can explain how you will deal with emergencies and actually define emergencies to make your team and clients more comfortable with changes.

Boundaries When You Work at Home

Some moms talked about boundaries with family and friends, especially work-from-home moms. (I feel like this is even more the case for entrepreneurs who work from home.) They can't simply have people stop by when kids are at school; it's their work time.

When you're working from home, you need to set the boundaries with your family. You want your family, both children and significant other, to respect your work space and your time. Establish the reasons you can be interrupted–the emergencies–or you will constantly find yourself shifting gears between things like disagreements between your children about a toy and trying to get back into work mode. My usual rule with my children is that someone needs to be hurt or it must be a situation they cannot solve. This doesn't mean situations they don't want to solve themselves. We usually go over the difference between an emergency and something they are upset about if I have a call or a deadline. That reminder in the moment helps.

I've been known to dangle a carrot for them, so they know they're working toward some sort of treat, if they let me get work done, especially when I'm working toward a deadline. If you work regularly from home when your children are around, find something that works for you, with or without the reward.

Boundaries and Your Areas of Interest

A cardiologist near San Francisco shared that she had to provide parameters for being able to say yes. For example, "I'm very interested in the project, but I can't do anything after 4 p.m. on Tuesday or Thursday." Essentially, if the colleague or potential collaborator couldn't work with her limited availability, then the answer is no. And she had to become okay with saying no to things she found interesting.

A dentist in Austin, Texas, volunteers at her children's school every other Wednesday, which is a day she traditionally has off. When other opportunities at the school come up, she can say yes or no, based on her work schedule and the personal and professional boundaries she has long put in place.

If you struggle with saying no, you're not alone. Realize that saying "no" to something means you're saying "yes" to something else. If you're struggling with how to say no, I have a few suggestions with phrasing that I use. One of these might be helpful in your situation.

First, saying no is a full statement. You don't need to explain yourself (most of the time). And, if you do explain yourself, make it short and sweet. For example, "I can't take this on because my schedule is full right now." And that is if you feel the need to include the "because my schedule is full" part.

Second, you can say "no" without using the actual word "no." Use phrases such as "I can't right now" or "I don't have time, but thank you for thinking of me." They say "no" politely, which might feel less abrupt.

And third, if you want to say "yes" to only part of what's being asked, then do that: "I can't do X, but I can do Y at this time." Nice and simple and enables you to participate in the part you care about.

If this is for specifically something at work, a phrase I have often used is, "I can do that instead of something else I'm working on for you. What can we move around (or what deadlines can we push back)?" Or something like, "I can start working on this and I'll work on the report I was already working on for you next week (or tomorrow or whatever timeframe is doable and accurate)." It reminds people that your time is limited and that you must juggle like everyone else.

If you're feeling guilty, remember that your time is one of your most important resources. You're trying to juggle a lot and make room for time with your family and for your work. Keep reminding yourself that you're saying yes to other areas in your life by saying no now. Or figure out what other things you can say no to, which are already on your plate, so that you can say yes to this.

I admit saying no is not a challenge for me. My own challenge in this area is that I want to say yes to several things and then I realize I have a lot more on my plate than I originally planned. I agreed when our younger son was born to not take on anything new without thinking through how it would impact all the other things I'm working on. And I usually end up talking things through with my husband, especially if it might impact family time. I highly recommend you think through the impact of saying yes as it relates to all the other things on your plate and that of your significant other, and even how it might impact your family.

Putting Boundaries in Place Now

If you need ideas on how to put boundaries in place, starting now, I have a few to share.

No Technology Times or Zones at Home

Try to set times when you walk away from technology when you're at home, unless it's an emergency. And no phones at the table during meals. Use this time for family members to connect with each other and not to someone on the other end of the phone. And this keeps older kids off of their phones too.

Response Time to Non-Emergency Communication

Look at when you respond to non-emergency communications, whether email, phone, or text. If it's always immediately, that might not be the best approach. We all want to acknowledge the people we work with, both internally and externally, and be considered responsive. Ask yourself if you need to answer back with an immediate response. Probably not. Consider a new rule about non-emergency communications within twenty-four hours, by end of day, or whatever time frame you're comfortable with. Give yourself some wiggle room, so that people don't expect you to respond in minutes and then keep contacting you until you do. You could be traveling, in an all-day meeting, sick, taking care of a sick child, or working on a major deadline.

Better Define Emergency Situations

If you're running into a lot of what appears to be emergencies for your clients or team, but isn't really an emergency, it might be time to define or redefine what an emergency is. Make sure everyone agrees to those definitions, both internally like your manager and team, and externally, such as clients and even vendors. Everyone you usually interact with needs to be on the same page about these definitions since they can vary from person to person or even project to project. If you need to change up the definition by project, have an initial call or summary page that everyone receives at the beginning of the project.

Tools to Help with Boundaries

You understand boundaries are important and you have some ideas of what you'd like to put in place. What about tools to help make it all come together?

Some moms suggested putting an email out of office response that includes the response time for all messages (e.g., Thank you for your message. I will respond in twenty-four hours.). It's an easy way for you to acknowledge people and let them know you'll get back to them in a reasonable amount of time. It can be included in contracts under a communications or response time section (you still want to highlight this early on as you start relationships with new clients and teams).

You can do the same in your outgoing voicemail that says you'll return the communication within a certain amount of time, such as by end of day or within twenty-four hours, which everyone agrees to ahead of time.

There are online tools you can put in place to limit your time on the internet or on social media so that you can focus on work for a set time. You can lock and unlock programs or devices after a specific amount of time has passed (e.g., no internet for thirty minutes or from 10 a.m. to 12 p.m.).

There are lots of different types of tools to help with boundaries; you need to decide what kinds of boundaries will help and research the tools available. And many of them are free or have a free version.

In summary:

Boundaries are important from a professional and personal perspective.

- Boundaries can improve your workflow.
- Having boundaries in place can help when it comes to areas of interest.
- It's important to implement boundaries the right way for you so that they help you and aren't simply an idea.

- There are technical tools to help with putting boundaries in place.

CHAPTER 12

OUTSOURCING

YOU'RE TRYING TO BE MORE productive and manage your time better. Perhaps it's time to outsource tasks or duties so that you can focus on what you do best. And, if that is the case, do you need to make changes to your personal support structure (e.g., sitter, housekeeper, etc.)? More than 10 percent of the moms I interviewed suggested getting help as a key piece of advice. That help might be a babysitter or sending your children to mothers' day out a few days a week or it could be a housekeeper. If you're an entrepreneur, this support structure could be someone or something on the business side, whether paying for a tool or virtual assistant or specialist.

Take a look at your current support structure and how you need to change it to facilitate more work-life balance. Keep in mind that you might have to get accustomed to any changes, so factor in an adjustment period.

One thing that came up time and time again is that if you work from home, and if you have young children who aren't yet in school, you will likely still need someone to watch them. That could be a part-time or nanny share, full-time nanny, au pair, babysitter, daycare, mothers' day out, preschool or Montessori program, to name a few. There are so many options. See which one of these works best for you if you need someone to care for younger children once you consider the pros and cons.

If care from outside of the home isn't an option for whatever reason, consider switching off days with another mom, so that both of you have time to do work without interruption. Be creative in how you find non-traditional care options like this. At times a fellow mom with boys about the same ages as mine and I switch off days with three-hour blocks, so that we can each work when we don't have the boys. You need dedicated time to get work done and it's hard to do with young children in the house.

Help with Household Chores

One of the top five recommendations from moms was to find help. And it happens that finding help with household duties was a top tip. Understand what you need, whether it's a housekeeper, nanny, help with cooking, or some combination, and find that person. Be specific in what you want that person to do when you're in the hiring process.

One of the ways an engineer at a petrochemical company in Houston has dealt with this challenge is to hire someone who is part nanny, housekeeper, and household manager to do the things that neither parent can get to. It has made their household function more efficiently, as you can imagine. And, everything gets done and both parents can continue to have their demanding careers. And the engineer's time after work and on the weekend is spent enjoying time with her kids and husband instead of doing all the household things that must be done, especially when they're not done during the week.

If you need help with these areas, but think that financially it's not feasible, see if some parts may be. Maybe even having someone come for an hour every week will help deal with an element of household chores like laundry, cleaning bathrooms, or mopping.

Know When to Outsource

Maybe you're realizing that you know you need help, but you don't know in which areas. In interviews, moms talked about knowing when it's time to ask for help. How do you know when to look for outside help or even what to outsource? There were a few key times and reasons when moms I spoke with knew it was time to bring in outside help.

Moms Lack Specific Skills

What if you don't have the skill to complete a task? I can't sew other than replacing a button. Thank goodness for my mother who can. If we need real sewing done, I'm not going to try and I'm OK with that. I'm handing it off to my mom (or to a professional).

In a day-to-day situation, what happens if you didn't learn to cook? You could get frozen meals or eat out every night. Or, if you're looking to be healthier, you could get prepared healthy meals delivered or even pay someone to cook meals in your home.

There is a resource out there for almost every skill you need. It's a matter of matching your needs with expert skills, price tag, and general preferences.

Tasks Are Too Time Consuming

Is there something that takes up a lot of time proportionate to your overall schedule? Again, meal preparation or maybe housekeeping might be one of these areas. Either you need to figure out how to be more efficient with these tasks or it might be time to consider outside help. (It could be that you need to do both–be more efficient and engage outside help.) There are lots of aspects of maintaining your home that you can outsource. And it doesn't need to be a professional service that you turn to for help. There might even neighborhood kids who are looking to make more money for things like yard service. A mother's helper can tidy up after the kids, which can sometimes feel like a full-time job (well, at least in my house with our two young boys).

Sometimes we can turn to our significant other or a family member, but that's not always an option. When busy times for my husband and me overlap, I might ask for a mother's helper to come one or two nights a week late in the day to heat up dinner and sit with our boys while they eat and help get them ready for bed. The other five or six nights we're eating dinner as a family, but those one or two nights, my husband and I are getting more done. It helps keep stress levels down. And after the boys are ready for bed and have heard a few stories, either my husband or I tuck them in. This can be a teenager in the neighborhood or a sitter we use regularly. I've even had a housekeeper come to only clean bathrooms, change sheets, and mop the floor. It's an hour, but that would have taken me hours of my time when I could be working. And it's a limited time during the year, so it's not cost prohibitive.

You Dread Household Duties

Is there something you cannot stand doing, even if you know how and even it's not that much time? For example, many moms I spoke with hire a housekeeper to come to their homes once a week or monthly. They realized that even with more time, housekeeping was still something they didn't want to do.

A branding strategist in Cody, Wyoming, shared that she doesn't enjoy meal planning, but that her sister is a caterer, and does the meal plan and the meal prep once groceries are purchased.

Many moms I know can't stand grocery shopping, which can also be time consuming. They have meals delivered, use services that plan meals and send the ingredients already portioned out, or buy groceries through an online service. There are all kinds of services in these categories, so you have options.

How to Find New Resources

The easiest way to find a new resource when you've realized you want to outsource tasks is to ask your tribe. Ask who helps them with specific tasks. Engage social media for this or simply send out an email or text. Try to be specific with what you need and even what you're wanting to pay. If your own network doesn't have the resources you need and want, ask the people you see each day such as your coworkers, clients, neighbors, or the parents you see at school. There is a high probability the resources are out there; you simply have to ask the right people the right questions.

In summary:

Figure out what you can outsource and find the right people or services to fill those needs to have better work-life balance.

- Know what you want to outsource.

- Know who to ask for help.

- Change who or what services are in your personal support structure to make this happen.

CHAPTER 13

WORK TRAVEL

WHEN I ASKED MY NETWORK about any additional topics they would like me to cover for this book, one came up that I hadn't talked about at all in the first *Mompowerment* book–traveling as a working mom. Since this is an area that I have no experience in, I reached out to moms who travel for work and got their advice and added additional advice that I found in my research.

Empower Others

You're about to travel and your child gets sick unexpectedly with a high fever, stomach bug, etc. You know, those illnesses that give you no warning. A marketing consultant for consumer packaged goods in Dallas, Texas, shares that there's "nothing you can do about it and dad, grandma, the nanny, or whoever [is in charge while you're gone] and your child will be just fine." Sometimes you must embrace that things are out of your hands and empower those who are part of your support network, including your significant other.

A marketing strategist and researcher in Austin, Texas, shares that she will sometimes give "dad a date night alone when [I'm] out of town" so that he has downtime while she's gone or she can also do it when she returns. Find out what your significant other needs and facilitate it with a babysitter and pay for it. It can be tough to do everything yourself when your significant other is traveling, especially if it's for long stretches.

Outsource What You Can

The Austin-based marketing strategist and researcher shares that she will often order "pre-made casseroles, so that meal prep is easy" while she's out of town. She also suggests, "Getting a morning or after school/evening sitter if you have a big family" to deal with "the crazy, frustrating parts of the day."

Logistics When You're Pumping

One of the hardest aspects of travel when you're a new mother is dealing with the logistics of pumping. There are many options out there, so consider what are you comfortable with, what will your company pay for, and what can you afford. For example, if you're going to be away for several days, will your company pay to send back your breast milk? There are several companies that do this very thing and you can find one that operates where you'll be and gives you best practices on packaging the milk. Your employer might not have considered doing this, so it never hurts to ask about the service for new mothers. Or your employer might not publicize it, but the company pays for a service, so, again, it never hurts to ask.

If you're traveling for longer stints, does it make more sense to bring your child? Will your company pay for you to bring along someone to help you, whether it's your significant other or another caregiver? And, if not, can you pay for that cost or maybe split it with your employer?

Or could you bring your child and find someone to help you at your destination? This option might make more sense if you're significant other also travels or if your caregiver can't come with you, especially if you seem to travel to the same places and have a base there. For example, I have friends who travel to see their clients regularly. It's always the same place and they have clients who also have children, so their clients would know local caregivers.

Be Intentional with Your Time Before You Leave

You don't want to sneak away when it's time to head out on a work trip. In the days before you go on your trip, have focused time with your kids. Get on the floor and play or have some mom/child dates doing something fun that you both enjoy. Leading up to your trip share what you'll be doing and who you'll be with.

Stay Connected While You Travel

It can be hard to explain to kids why mommy will be away, especially if you must travel a lot for work. What if you had them be part of it? Look on a map to see where you're headed and talk about where you're going. Talk about sites in the city, what food the city is known for, the weather, etc. Tell them the names of your teammates and/or your clients. Make sure they know it's not for fun and they're not missing out.

Write out some notes before you leave and have whoever is watching the kids give a note (or read a note if the kids are too young) while you're gone. Maybe put it in their lunchbox. (I put notes in my older son's lunchbox since he can read them and occasionally put in a joke, which was a great idea I heard from a friend.) Maybe try to do a stack of these before you leave so that they go in the lunchbox while you're out of town. Sure, it takes a bit of forethought, but it's worth it.

When you're away, use an online tool so that you're face to face when you chat. Show them your hotel room, what you're walking by, what's for dinner, etc. Call to say good morning and/or good night.

Get some notes from your significant other, nanny, grandma, the sitter, or whoever is taking care of the kids to see what specifically you can ask the kids about from that day, so that you're engaged with what's going on. Talk to each child separately, so that they have a bit of mommy time, albeit super short mommy time.

Consider taking a book that they love and actually reading your kids' bedtime story while you're away. Or maybe get a new book that they don't know. It could even be a book about the place where you're traveling. What a fun treat to get a new book and hear mommy's voice! You can always get a second copy so that they can follow at home if you like.

Lean on Your Support System

I'll share more about the importance of your tribe in the Chapter 14, but this is another thing that is incredibly important. When you need help from your tribe, whoever that includes for your specific situation, ask for the help. Chances are your tribe will be able to help you and it will certainly help with lowering your stress level when you're about to get on a plane or aren't even in the same city to deal with what life throws your way. But people don't know to help–even people you know well–until you ask.

Coming Home Rituals

Some of my friends give something specific to their kids like a stuffed animal when they return from their travels. I don't want to add to our toy collection without reason, so I usually give a T-shirt and/or a keychain since it's something my boys and their classmates collect. Why not have some cool unique ones, right?

What about doing a fun activity when you return. I took lunch to the boys' schools the next day when I was out of town for several days in a row. The boys loved it! It wasn't about a thing, but about spending a few extra minutes together in the middle of the day for our older son. Our younger son felt like he got an unexpected treat and that made him feel really special.

What Happens if You Enjoy Work Travel?

What if you're one of those moms who actually enjoys the work travel that you do? You like your job and your clients and you're excited to spend time with them. Great! There is nothing wrong with being excited about getting to travel for work. There is no guilt necessary in motherhood. Ever! Feel fortunate that you enjoy your career and that you have a good enough relationship with your clients that you're excited to spend time with them. That is a great feeling!

And don't forget that you'll also likely get points from hotel and airline travel when you do this regularly. You can talk to your children about helping plan a fun trip where you go as a family because mommy travels for work. What a treat!

If you are dealing with mommy guilt, I share more about combating mommy guilt in Chapter 16.

In summary:

For those working moms who find themselves traveling for work, get some ideas on making the process smoother for you and your family.

- Empower others to help, whether it's through outsourcing or reaching out to your tribe.
- Understand the logistics of pumping while you travel for work.
- Be intentional with your time before you leave.

- Stay in touch while you're gone.

- Create rituals for when you come home.

- Don't feel guilty if you enjoy work travel.

PART V

THE PERSONAL SIDE OF WORK-LIFE BALANCE

CASE STUDY: Creating a Lifestyle You Love

After working about ten years in various industries and roles, a business coach for women entrepreneurs found clarity in her life and business after becoming a mother. Her journey after college started with interior design, a field in which she found quite a bit of success. She admits it was hard to walk away from a successful business, but it wasn't quite the right fit. She kept looking at roles and industries.

She realized that she liked creating the infrastructure for businesses, such as the processes and strategies. Somewhere in the middle of all of the business stuff, she got a yoga certification and taught yoga. And then she had her first child, which helped all the pieces come together. Her mindful approach from her yoga practice married nicely with her approach to business coaching for women entrepreneurs. With a focus on family and a balanced lifestyle, she designed and structured her business to function part time. Her mindset shift was how to be professionally successful while working three days per week.

And with the birth of her second daughter, she is able to maintain this approach. No question, this business coach loves her lifestyle. She's able to do something she loves professionally and be a strong presence in her daughters' lives. While some people put their lives on hold to build their business, she has enjoyed the journey of raising a family while building a business.

Children can help working moms prioritize and put reasonable expectations on you and your career. She gets to create the lifestyle and career she wants and can attain a six-figure salary.

Her advice for anyone interested in working part time as part of your overall work-life balance:

- *Create your vision of what you're looking for.* Understand what you want out of your career. Look at what you want your schedule to be. Take time to plan out how you want the two to work together.

- *Seek outside help if you need it.* Know what kind of outside resources will actually help you and address any needs you may have. Be comfortable with asking for that help.

- *Include time for self-care.* If you're only focused on others, whether at home or work, you'll get to a point where you have nothing left to give. Build self-care time into your day, especially if you find yourself fighting burnout at work.

- *Understand what you need when you're transitioning to a part-time role.* Create support practices and make sure to build yourself up when transitioning to the part-time career approach. You want to make sure you are feeling your best when you make the transition, so you set yourself up for success.

CHAPTER 14

WORKING MOMS NEED A TRIBE

ABOUT 10 PERCENT OF MOMS, both entrepreneurs and those who work for an employer, shared the advice of finding help. Some moms talked about help for the personal side of things, others talked about help on the professional side, and some suggested help in both areas.

Let's be honest, it can be hard to ask for help. Is that because we feel like it's a sign of weakness? Do we feel that we must be super-moms (and what does that even mean anyway)? If we're the one who others have turned to for help, do we hesitate to ask for help for our needs? Or maybe it's simply that we don't know who to ask for help.

The saying is that raising a child takes a village. Many of the moms I interviewed used this phrase, whether referring to help at home or at work. Let's talk about creating your village because that will make life easier for all working moms.

Importance of Your Tribe

Some people are naturally part of a tribe. Sometimes it's your actual family or even those you grew up with. Some aren't as lucky and they need to find their tribe. No question, a tribe is important. Remember what we said earlier about it takes a village? There were countless moms who I interviewed who shared they would not be able to work without their tribe. A lawyer in the Atlanta area said it simply, "I know my village is backing me up. I couldn't have raised my daughter and worked . . . without my village."

What do I mean by tribe, you might ask? These are people whom you have a deep connection with and are part your personal support system. They are the people we turn to, whether for help when things come up, advice, moral support, as a cheerleader to celebrate our successes, and so much more. Your tribe can include family, neighbors, friends, and your support system (e.g., housekeeper, babysitter, or nanny). Whoever you want to include in your tribe is your decision, but make sure you have one. Don't be afraid to ask these people for help and think outside of the box.

There are times when as moms we feel like we're going through something unique when we have hard moments. That's largely because we don't usually talk about the challenges of motherhood. We want to make sure that our situation is normal and talk through daily hiccups or huge challenges, or simply get advice based on another woman or mom's experience. I can't say the number of times I asked a friend, whose kids are slightly older than mine, about how to deal with a situation. And sometimes I talk to moms with kids the same age as mine to get a different perspective.

We all have our hard moments–monumental meltdowns, moments of extreme toddler independence, family illness, marital challenges, or even the times we feel like we're not enough as a mom, employee or entrepreneur, or as a friend. And there are so many more times when we need to be able to reach out and talk to someone in person, on the phone, or even online. It's much easier to deal with these tough moments and even the day-to-day hiccups when we have a tribe to turn to. (If you're struggling with finding your tribe, think about using the information on networking from Chapter 7 to help find like-minded people.)

Your Tribe and Childcare

These are people you trust, so would you trust them with your children? I would trust my tribe with my children without any hesitation.

One great tip that a few moms shared in their interviews was to trade off with trusted friends and neighbors for childcare needs. Set up a schedule so that you watch your kids and hers for a time and she does the same for you another day. It doesn't have to be a full day of care. It can be a few hours at a time, but that can be a lot of time to get work done without interruption. Or that might be time to exercise or take a moment for self-care (there are times when you really need a moment to yourself and a friend can step in to help you and let you take that moment), or you can meal prep for the week without paying someone to watch your children. This approach of trading childcare makes sense for both moms. It's a win-win!

Working Playdates

Even though my kids are in preschool and elementary school five days a week, I feel like there are still so many days I have to cover when kids are out of school. My clients still expect me to meet deadlines, even with the random days when kids are home. Can you relate?

How about engaging your tribe to do a working playdate? I mentioned networking playdates in Chapter 7 and working playdates are similar in many ways. When you're trying to get things done and kids are either not school age yet or have those random days off like teacher workdays or school holidays, consider a working playdate. The kids are entertained and likely having fun with limited effort from moms, and moms get stuff done. It's also great to do during summer and winter breaks when parents are trying to figure out what to do with kids.

There are ways to make this a smoother interaction so that you get to keep working and kids get to have fun (and this combo is the whole point, right?). You can follow the guidelines to the networking playdates from Chapter 7 and also consider the following since a great place to do these is at someone's house:

- You either need to be disciplined enough to not chat while you're in the same room or have two quiet work spaces. You want both work spaces to be equally desirable. For example, you don't want one space to be in a quiet room and the other to be in a spot where kids will run around and interrupt or distract you. If they aren't equally quiet, as the hostess, take the less desirable location. (Hint: If you plan on doing these regularly and don't have two quiet spaces, consider a good pair of noise cancelling headphones.)

- Take care of logistics upfront if you're the hostess. Explain the rules of the house at the beginning (e.g., no running on the stairs, no drinks and food outside of the breakfast area, etc.). You never know what rules look like in other homes so don't make assumptions that kids know what they should or shouldn't do in your home. Make sure everyone knows where to find snacks (yep, you need to have snacks for everyone) and drinks (or easy access to cups for water). Show everyone where the bathroom is. (Maybe consider putting something special on the door handle since kids can often wait until the last minute and might struggle to find the restroom).

In summary:

Creating a support network is important to working moms.

- Your tribe, whoever that includes, is important, especially when you're a working mom.

- Consider engaging your tribe for a working playdate.

.

CHAPTER 15

WORKING MOTHERS AND SELF-CARE

Take Care of Yourself

Some of you who are reading this might be really good at taking care of yourself, including eating well, exercising, and getting enough sleep. If you're like most moms, taking care of yourself falls off the to-do list regularly.

Taking better care of yourself includes making healthier food choices. I won't turn this into a lecture on eating well, but I will remind you that what you eat fuels you or it simply fills you up (and it might not even really do this). When you're fueling your body, you likely feel better and are more energized, right? Find ways to have a breakfast that fills you up. You want to have lunch options that are healthy and that you enjoy. Take time to figure those options out and actually include them in your diet (and by diet I mean eating habit and not your attempt at losing weight). And while you're at it with trying to eat healthier, don't forget to drink enough water throughout the day.

Slow down and take time to eat. Yes, several moms I interviewed eat lunch at their desk, but that still means they can enjoy what they're eating. And, so can you. You don't have make it a five-course meal, but you can enjoy the short (or long) time you have.

I understand how busy you are, but you still need exercise and sleep. I'm coming at this from the perspective of a busy, working mom, like you.

I'm going to talk about exercise a bit differently than a trainer or fitness coach. When it comes to exercise, I'm sure we all know that exercising three, four, or, yes, seven days a week for thirty minutes or more each day is ideal. I understand that. I also understand that can be hard to fit in when you're a working mom. So, instead of skipping your thirty-minute workout because you can't fit it all in, try a different approach. It's something I've been doing for more than a year and a half and it has made a big difference. I exercise whenever and for however long I can. It can add up to thirty minutes throughout the day. Or if it doesn't, fifteen minutes is better than nothing. And, if I fit in longer stretches, that's great! And if not, I let the short bursts of exercise add up.

And don't forget to sleep. At some point, refueling yourself requires sleep–turning everything off and getting into bed to let your body recoup. I won't say it must be a certain number of hours, but work on getting the right amount of sleep for your own needs.

Your Self-care Routine

We will spend the time doing what's necessary for our kids, significant other, parents, neighbors, volunteering obligations, etc., but what about spending time on ourselves? So many of the moms I interviewed talked about the need as a working mom to take time for self-care. Their message is clear–we need to make time to fill our cups. Self-care makes each of us be a better mom, significant other, friend, sibling, colleague, neighbor, you name it.

How can we be at our best when we often turn away from taking care of ourselves? It might even sound counterintuitive, but think about it. How can we take care of others with our full energy and be present if we're not at our best? And that is mental, physical, emotional–a holistic version of–care. As one mom describes it, "I'm happier and it trickles down to my kids, who are also happier."

It doesn't have to be a visit to the spa, unless that is what you want. I'm referring to self-care as a consistent part of life, so that we don't feel drained over time and unhappy with ourselves and those around us. By that point, it can be harder to be present and happy with our families and our work.

So how can we bring self-care into our day when we're so busy? The answer to that is very personal. It's what you need, not what your sister, friend, neighbor, or anyone else needs. Remember, we're not trying to be perfect; we're trying to be our best self. That's all we can ask for, right? Here are a few things to consider when you're figuring out your self-care routine:

- What makes you happy, outside of family and potentially work stuff? What is it about that thing that makes you happy? How else does it make you feel (e.g., light, fun, calm, energized, etc.)?

- Is there an activity that makes you smile, even just thinking about it? What is it about that activity that you enjoy?

- Can you think of an image that gets you to think happy thoughts? Where are you? What are you doing?

- What's something you can do to help you integrate small moments of self-care in your day or week?

- What can you do to integrate big moments of self-care into your day or week?

- What's one thing that immediately changes your mood (e.g., dancing, laughing, etc.)?

- When you think of relaxing or filling your cup, what does that look like?

I've given ideas for figuring out what fills your cup, but really, it can be anything–a nap, writing in a journal, talking a walk, reading a book, connecting with a friend, taking a bubble bath, or even something more luxurious like a spa outing. Anything that helps fill your cup can be part of your self-care routine. And the way we want to fill our cup can vary from day to day or even throughout the day.

You might say you don't have time for self-care on a regular basis, so try something once a week. Or consider rethinking what you do for self-care daily. I do a morning self-care check-in before I even get out of bed. I see how I'm feeling and what adjustments I need to make for the day.

For example, if I'm tired, I may need to give myself more time to get things done (and not press the snooze button) or maybe take something off my to-do list that isn't necessary today. Maybe I'm feeling stressed because of looming deadlines, so I know to breathe more. Even when I'm super excited about something, I know it can impact my family if they aren't feeling that same excitement. It's a small thing, but it makes a difference for me and those I've suggested it to. It enables me to have better interactions with my family, clients, friends, and colleagues throughout the day.

Another simple thing is taking deep breaths. We're not talking heavy breathing. I'm talking breaths from your diaphragm. It only takes a few minutes of deep breaths to get the benefit.

If you're more visual, create something like an inspiration board with images of things you love. Maybe you have pictures from a recent trip somewhere that you really enjoyed. Include a few snapshots of places you visited or want to visit. Let your mind wander as you look at your board and enjoy the moment. Imagine yourself there. You don't have to have an entire inspiration board. It can even be a picture or two that allows you to find that happy place for a moment or two.

And, as much as I think it's important to find simple moments of self-care each day, you shouldn't hesitate to take a day or two or ten for your self-care, if that's what you need. That means getting away from the day-to-day obligations and family. Maybe it will be more fun with a good friend or in a group. The idea is to enjoy the day or weekend or week, letting everything else fall away. And, again, make it what you want and need. Figure out how to fill your cup and do that thing.

Keep in mind that these are ideas and you might have something that's already working for you. Do whatever is right for your own needs and make sure to integrate a bit of that into your week and, I hope, into your day.

What's Stopping You?

I've shared why it's important to include self-care in your routine, especially as a busy, working mom. And even how to figure out what you can do for self-care, if you don't know already. I gave examples and even shared my own self-care rituals, some of which only take minutes.

So, here's my question to you. What's stopping you from integrating self-care into your day or week? Is it not enough time? Do you need to use your time better? Can you make adjustments in your to-do list such as delegating? Are there things you can remove from your list, because some things don't have to get done today or this week? Are you simply trying to do too much in a day and setting an unreasonable expectation of your time?

Are you limiting your definition of self-care? Remember, you don't need hours, so see how you might be able to fit small moments of self-care into your busy day. If you want to go big, schedule it on your calendar and make sure nothing gets in the way of that self-care day or week.

Are you not sure if it's worth your time or if you have earned it? I can tell you already that it is and that you've more than earned it. Mama, let me remind you that you're doing your best. And you deserve a moment to yourself. Honestly, you deserve hours and days for your self-care, but moments are likely what you can fit in to your busy life. Put it on the calendar if that's what it takes because remember that your calendar reflects what it is you value.[1]

And, if that's still a struggle, maybe it's time for an accountability self-care buddy (AKA a good friend). Have a friend keep you accountable so that you consistently take time for self-care or simply do the self-care with your friend. Sometimes we need a friend to keep our best interest in mind and remind us to do the same.

Take that moment to fill your cup. Take as many moments as you need and want to fill your cup. You want it. You need it. You've earned it. Enjoy it!

In summary:

We all need self-care as part of our usual routine.

- Make healthy food choices and drink water.

- Exercise and get enough sleep.

- If you don't already know how to fill your cup, explore different ways to do this.

- Schedule your self-care moments into your day if you need to.

- Consider a self-care accountability buddy to help you get more self-care in your day or week.

EASY SELF-CARE IDEAS

◆ Write in a journal

◆ Meditate

◆ Take deep breaths

◆ Read, watch, or look at something that makes you belly laugh

◆ Morning self-care check-in

◆ Read a book for pleasure for at least six minutes

◆ Go for a walk

◆ Take a nature walk or hike

◆ Coffee, lunch, dinner, or happy hour with a friend

◆ Chat with a friend on the phone

◆ Take a bubble bath

◆ Put on a face mask

◆ Listen to music to help you relax

◆ Have a dance party to music that gives you energy

◆ Take a nap

◆ Do some gardening

CHAPTER 16

MANAGING MOMMY GUILT

A TOPIC THAT COMES UP TIME and time again in my conversations with working moms and in a few interviews is mommy guilt. I will admit that mommy guilt is not something that I personally struggle with. I understand that most moms deal with it, sometimes daily or even several times a day. I don't judge the moms who feel its pull and I hope they don't judge me.

There are three things that seem to keep my mommy guilt at bay. First, our initial experience with school for our older son (and subsequently for our younger son) has been amazing. Second, I understand what I need and what our boys need. And finally, my being a working mom is all our boys have ever known, which has helped manage expectations on all sides.

What Does Your Child Need?

When our older son was about fifteen months old, we took him with us to look at mothers' day out programs (essentially half-day preschool for younger kids), so that I could have more consistent time to work. He thought it was amazing that there was a place with kid-sized stuff and toys everywhere. He loved the idea of playing with classmates his age a few days a week. For us, the challenge was that he didn't want to leave and we had to wait about three months to come back for the start of the school year.

When his school finally started that fall, he was eighteen months old. He was so excited that first day that he walked into the classroom without even giving me a hug or saying goodbye. The other nine children in his class were crying and he walked in and started playing. I was sad for about a minute until the teacher whispered to me, "You need to leave right now," as she attempted to keep our son smiling, while consoling nine unhappy, crying children with the help of her teacher's aide.

I might have felt more guilt over time if his teacher wouldn't have been like another grandmother, providing such a loving environment where our son learned so much each day he attended. My theory is that his continued enthusiasm about school and learning six years later is largely because of the amazing experiences he had from the very beginning, spending Tuesdays and Thursdays with his loving teachers, 9 a.m.-1:30 p.m.

He continued to have amazing teachers, who he adored, throughout preschool. He loves to learn and take it all in like a sponge. And he is very social and talks about the interactions with friends and all the fun stuff they're doing. Keeping him out of school would have been unkind on my part. I wouldn't have been able to mimic the learning and social environment at home, even with playdates and teaching him new things. His preschool teachers provided activities that I wouldn't have come up with on my own.

In fact, we found out how incredibly enthusiastic he is about school when he started kindergarten in fall 2016. The first few weeks of school, he was waking up at 4:45 or 5 each morning. That went on for the first two or three weeks because he was *that excited* about going to school. The added challenge was that he was waking up our

191 | MANAGING MOMMY GUILT

then almost three-year-old. It's a long day when you've been up since 4:45 a.m. with two young children. I finally had to sit him down and explain that school doesn't open at 5 a.m. or even 6 a.m. and that he might not be able to learn as much as his classmates if he is too tired. Thankfully, that worked. Let's hope this passion for school continues.

We're taking the same path with our younger son, who also loves school so far. He talks about his teachers and the activities he does in class. He asks about his teachers and classmates on the weekends. It's amazing to watch. I won't lie, it's wonderful to know that you leave your child in the hands of teachers they adore, who are loving and enthusiastic with the kids they teach. I know we're fortunate and that has helped remove any guilt I might have felt if things were different. I might have abandoned my professional opportunities if my boys were crying every day at drop-off. But, thankfully that's not the case.

Since I know my children and their enthusiasm about school, I don't feel guilty about their time there. I decided that my kids' needs include going to school and that is good for them and for me.

How can you use this? Think through what your child needs. If he or she is having fun, learning, and enjoying the school or day-care experience, isn't that what's important? Maybe reframing things with this in mind that can help minimize some of your mommy guilt.

What Do You Need?

On the flip side, it's helpful to consider your needs. I need to work to keep my sanity. I am a go-getter and am very goal-oriented. Setting goals related to work and achieving them is important to me. I need work to counter-balance my family life. I don't feel guilt for wanting this balance between career and family.

I'm not alone in feeling this way. A mom in event sales in At-lanta described the situation perfectly: "Some moms are made to be

SAHMs and some are made to work outside of the home. I need a break and I need social interaction with adults." And this is key. This mom knows herself and knows what she needs and embraces it.

A Chicago-based language expert who teaches young children and adults described her approach as, "Don't let guilt 'haunt' you." She encourages moms to understand their professional needs and feel empowered to make decisions based on those needs.

If you want or need to work be at peace with that. You are still likely spending a lot of time with your kids when they aren't in school. You're still making the effort to have the work-life balance that you need and that's all you can ask of yourself.

I can't imagine having the patience to manage my child's learning over time. I can teach and reinforce some skills, but not provide a homeschool environment. That is not my strength. I know myself and I know my strengths and being my children's primary teacher is not one of them.

Work When Kids are Young

The final thing I will share that helps with managing mommy guilt is that I've always worked, other than maternity leave. My working is all my boys have ever known. I even started our younger son in the baby room at the mothers' day out program so that I could have dedicated time to work.

It's Personal

For most of the moms I spoke with and in my own case, it's important to understand your own situation and to figure out what works for you and your family. It's very personal and it's largely about your individual perspective and needs, both professionally and personally. Take the time to think through what will work in your situation for you and your family. Leave the guilt out of the equation and be comfortable with the decisions you make for your career and family, and the balance in between.

Don't Compare Yourself to the Joneses

If you focus on what others are doing, whether SAHMs or working moms, you will likely feel guilty about your approach or about what you're not doing right. In part, that guilt might be driven by feelings of not doing enough, especially in an age when we see so much perfection in social media. Don't compare your situation to others, because each situation is different. You never know what the next mom isn't focusing energy on that you are. And who knows what happened a few minutes before and after the perfect moment you see online or in a holiday card, or hear about at the PTA meeting. And, from what I see with other moms, the more you compare to other moms and family situations, the more likely you are to feel guilty.

Give Yourself Some Grace

As much pressure as we might put on ourselves, we must remember to be kind and give ourselves some grace. It won't be perfect and that's fine. Own your strengths and be comfortable with "good enough." If you feel the need to be amazing in all areas of your life all the time, be kind to yourself if that doesn't happen.

Change the Definition

If you feel you must have it all, maybe it's time to change the definition of "having it all." Make the definition of what success looks like to you a personal one and include the pieces you find most important. Again, don't compare to others or use their definition. Don't look at your friends or colleagues, or what a magazine or book says.

Only you know what's most important to you and your family. You get to define, create your terms, and set your priorities. And, it's not something you set and it stays consistent, so allow for some flexibility. You have the flexibility and the permission to redefine these over time, because it can all change.

Mommy Guilt in the Interviews

An Austin-based make-up artist shared that she feels mommy guilt because she might miss her children's activities due to work. Her schedule is known months in advance, and kids' events get scheduled after the work calendar is already set. She doesn't want to disappoint her kids and have them feel she doesn't support what they're doing.

The owner of an advertising and marketing business in Austin, Texas, feels a "bit of guilt because she is always connected, since she needs to be accessible by her clients." She is always available to clients, but she isn't always working. She feels guilty for being connected and for the times when she does have to work.

These might be similar to your own situation. What can you do to feel less guilty about your own situation? Can you put more boundaries in place? Can you better define what is an appropriate reason for your team or a client to reach out after hours? Is there a way you can set expectations with your child for the times when you do have to work for a bit when you would usually play? What might help to decrease the guilt that you might feel when you must stay connected?

The most common reason for mommy guilt in the interviews was when things had to change unexpectedly, usually for a unique work situation. I understand that this can be tough for a child to understand. Sure, these unusual situations are inconvenient for you and your family, but remember that they aren't usually going to break everything you've created in your work-life balance.

In summary:

Managing mommy guilt is made easier by:

- Understanding your needs and those of your family;

- Redefining what having it all means;

- Not comparing your own situation to anyone else's; and

- Being kind to yourself when things are out of balance.

FINAL THOUGHTS

I WROTE THIS BOOK TO EMPOWER MOMS with knowledge and tools to think differently about work-life balance. And I've shared tips and advice from the amazing working moms who shared their stories with me from across the US in all sorts of industries. I hope you have grabbed several ideas from here to implement quickly in your own life or to take ideas from and make adjustments so that these ideas do fit in your life.

You are not alone in your interest in creating more work-life balance. And, chances are that if you work at a large company, there are probably other moms who are asking these same questions around the same time you are. What if you went to management as a group and started talking about changes in work-life balance instead of having one-off conversations with managers or senior leadership, with each mom negotiating individually? Think about the power of larger groups in negotiating, influencing, and driving change, instead of the power of one.

If you're the first mom at your employer who wants more flexibility in how you spend your day, start the conversations with your manager and senior leadership. Start asking the questions and start sharing answers with others around you. Begin the path and lead the way; don't shy away because you're first. Help employers provide you with support as you figure out and articulate what you want and need. Someone must lead the way. Maybe that person is you in this case. Be a trailblazer and embrace that you can open doors for other moms behind you.

If you decide that entrepreneurship is your path, feel empowered to take on clients who understand your version of work-life balance. Be confident in your skills and knowledge and know that will attract the right clients, in the short- and / or long-term. Build your business and don't get discouraged. I always tell my boys when we're doing something tough, "Slow and steady." Build your business how you want and be secure in your decision.

Pay it forward. Mentor and sponsor women that follow your path. Share tips and tools that work for you with other working moms. Hire moms as workers and embrace work-life balance and flexibility in how you treat them.

As a manager or leader in a company, enable your own team to think differently about their productivity and time management. Start asking what working moms want and need. Implement those ideas. Empower working moms to think differently about time management and support flexibility.

And, if you're an employer who couldn't create more flexibility so you had seasoned and strong employees leave to start their own business, what about using their services? They know your company and understand your needs intimately. They could be incredibly productive freelancers or consultants who you can tap into. Show them that they aren't alone in their endeavor to find work-life balance.

If we stopped considering ourselves alone on this journey and came together as a group, we are more likely to make major shifts happen. We can empower each other to find the work-life balance that we each we want. It's doable. We must start the conversations and the change will become inevitable.

Remember to head to www.mompowerment.com/booktemplates to download templates to help you on your path to greater work-life balance.

The Mompowerment Guide to Work-life Balance and Your Tribe

You might not be the only one in your tribe struggling with creating better work-life balance. If that's the case, buy a book for your sister, friend, neighbor, or whoever is struggling, and work on the exercises together. There is no question that it's helpful to be able to talk to someone about the ideas that you might come up with as you read this book. Who better than to talk to someone in your tribe! Make the conversations happen and share solutions that you're figuring out. Be a resource if they reach out for guidance.

END NOTES

Chapter 1

1   Gretchen Livingston and Kristen Bialik, "7 Facts about U.S. Moms," Fact Tank: News in the Numbers, Pew Research Center, Washington, D.C., May 10, 2018, http://www.pewresearch.org/fact-tank/2018/05/10/facts-about-u-s-mothers/.

Chapter 2

1   Kenneth Mathos, Ellen Galinsky, and James T. Bond, "National Study of Employers," (Alexandria, VA: Society for Human Resource Management, 2016), 23, http://whenworkworks.org/downloads/2016-National-Study-of-Employers.pdf.

2   Mathos, Galinsky, and Bond, "National Study of Employers," 26.

3   Chris Weller, "These 10 Countries Have the Best Parental Leave Policies in the World," Business Insider, August 22, 2013, http://www.businessinsider.com/countries-with-best-parental-leave-2016-8/.

4   Center on the Developing Child, "Five Numbers to Remember about Early Childhood Development (Brief)," Center on the Developing Child, 2009, http://developingchild.harvard.edu/resources/five-numbers-to-remember-about-early-childhood-development/.

5   Center on the Developing Child, "Five Numbers to Remember."

6   D'Vera Cohn and Paul Taylor, "Baby Boomers Approach 65–Glumly," Pew Research Center: Social and Demographic Trends, Washington, D.C., December 20, 2010, http://www.pewsocialtrends.org/2010/12/20/baby-boomers-approach-65-glumly.

7   Lisa Rabasca Roepe, "Are Gen X Women Being Squeezed Out of the Workplace?," Fast Company, December 15, 2015, https://www.fastcompany.com/3054410/are-gen-x-women-being-squeezed-out-of-the-workplace.

8   Roepe, "Are Gen X Women."

9   Roepe, "Are Gen X Women."

10   Roepe, "Are Gen X Women."

11   BridgeWorks, "Generation X 101," BridgeWorks, February 21, 2017.

12   BridgeWorks, "Generation X 101."

13   BridgeWorks, "Generation X 101."

14   BridgeWorks, "Generation X 101."

15   Roepe, "Are Gen X Women."

16   The Sage Group, Survey Report: 2015 Sage State of the Startup (Irvine, CA: The Sage Group, 2015), https://www.sage.com/na/~/media/site/sagena/responsive/docs/startup/report.

17   BridgeWorks., "Generation X 101."

18   PriceWaterhouseCoopers, Millennials at Work: Reshaping the Workplace (New York, NY: PriceWaterhouseCoopers, 2011), 8, accessed June 15, 2017, http://www.pwc.com/gx/en/managing-tomorrows-people/future-of-work/assets/reshaping-the-workplace.pdf.

19   Teresa Meek, "Work/Life Balance: What It Means to Millennials," Coca-Cola Journey, October 1, 2014, http://www.coca-colacompany.com/stories/work-life-balance-what-it-means-to-millennials.

20   Meek, "Work/Life Balance."

21   Jacquelyn Smith, "13 Things Successful Millennials Do in Their Spare Time," Business Insider, July 24, 2014, http://www.businessinsider.com/successful-millennials-spare-time-2014-7.

22   Richard Fry, "Millennials Surpass Gen Xers as the Largest Generation in U.S. Labor Force," Fact Tank: News in Numbers, Pew Research Center, Washington, D.C., May 11, 2015, http://www.pewresearch.org/fact-tank/2015/05/11/millennials-surpass-gen-xers-as-the-largest-generation-in-u-s-labor-force/.

Chapter 3

1   Nikki Graf, "Most Americans Say Children Are Better Off with a Parent at Home," Fact Tank: News in the Numbers, Pew Research Center, Washington, D.C., October 10, 2016, http://www.pewresearch.org/fact-tank/2016/10/10/most-americans-say-children-are-better-off-with-a-parent-at-home/.

2   Working Mother Research Institute, Breadwinning Moms: The Working Mother Report (New York: Bonner Corporation, 2016), 4, http://www.workingmother.com/sites/workingmother.com/files/attachments/2016/04/breadwinningmoms.pdf.

3   Kathleen L. McGinn, Elizabeth Long Lingo, and Mayra Cruz Castro, "Mums the Word! Cross-National Effects of Maternal Employment on Gender Inequalities at Work and at Home," Harvard Business School Working Paper, no. 15-094, June 2015 (Revised July 2015), 19-20, https://dash.harvard.edu/bitstream/handle/1/16727933/15-094%20(2).pdf?sequence=4.

4   McGinn, Lingo, and Castro, "Mums the Word!", 18.

5   McGinn, Lingo, and Castro, "Mums the Word!", 18-19.

6   McGinn, Lingo, and Castro, "Mums the Word!", 20.

7   McGinn, Lingo, and Castro, "Mums the Word!", 28.

Chapter 4

1   PL+US: Paid Leave for the United States, "Forging Ahead or Falling Behind? Paid Family Leave at America's Top Companies," Paid Leave for the United States, November 16, 2016, https://d3n8a8pro7vhmx.cloudfront.net/plus/pages/48/attachments/original/1480616519/report.pdf?1480616519.

2   "Family," PWC/United States, 2015-2017, http://www.pwc.com/us/en/about-us/diversity/pwc-family-support.html.

3   Rachel Gillett, "20 Great Places for Moms to Work," Business Insider, June 15, 2015, http://www.businessinsider.com/the-best-places-for-new-moms-to-work-2015-6.

Chapter 8

1   Sylvia Ann Hewlett, "The Right Way to Find a Career Sponsor," Harvard Business Review, September 11, 2013, https://hbr.org/2013/09/the-right-way-to-find-a-career-sponsor.

2   Sava Berhané, "Why Women Need Career Sponsors More Than Mentors," Fast Company, August 28, 2015, https://www.fastcompany.com/3050430/why-women-need-career-sponsors-more-than-mentors.

3   Geri Stengel, "Sponsorship: Why Entrepreneurs Should Take a Page from the Corporate Playbook," Forbes, June 12, 2013, https://www.forbes.com/sites/geristengel/2013/06/12/sponsorship-why-entrepreneurs-should-take-a-page-from-the-corporate-playbook.

4   Stengel, "Sponsorship: Why Entrepreneurs Should."

5   Stengel, "Sponsorship: Why Entrepreneurs Should."

6   Berhané. "Why Women Need Career."

7   Sylvia Ann Hewlett, "Make Yourself Sponsor-Worthy," Harvard Business Review, February 6, 2014, https://hbr.org/2014/02/make-yourself-sponsor-worthy.

8   Hewlett, "Make Yourself Sponsor-Worthy."

Chapter 9

1   United States Small Business Administration Office of Advocacy, "Small Business Profile," The Small Business Advocate 35, no. 1 (March-April 2016): 3, https://www.sba.gov/sites/default/files/March_April_2016_FINAL_508_compliant.pdf.

2   United States Small Business Administration Office of Advocacy, "Small Business Profile," 3.

3   Arnobio Morelix, Victor Hwang, and Inara S. Tareque, State of Entrepreneurship 2017. Zero Barriers: Three Mega Trends Sharing Future of Entrepreneurship (Kansas City, MO: Ewing Marion Kauffman Foundation, 2017), 9, http://www.kauffman.org/~/

media/kauffman_org/resources/2017/state_of_entrepreneurship_address_report_2017.pdf.

4   Womenable, "The 2016 State of Women-Owned Business Report," American Express OPEN, April 2016, http://about.americanexpress.com/news/docs/2016x/2016SWOB.pdf.

5   Womenable, "The 2016 State of Women-Owned."

6   First Round Capital, First Round 10-year project, n.d., accessed April 4, 2017, http://10years.firstround.com/.

7   Marisa LaScala, "It's Small Business Week–Remember the Mompreneurs," Working Mother, May 5, 2015, http://www.workingmother.com/content/small-business-week-remember-mompreneurs.

8   First Round Capital, First Round 10-year project.

Chapter 10

1   Shana Lebowitz, "Here's How the 40-Hour Workweek Became the Standard in America," Business Insider, October 24, 2015, http://www.businessinsider.com/history-of-the-40-hour-workweek-2015-10.

2   Lebowitz, "Here's How the 40-Hour."

3   Douglas Brinkley, "The 40-hour Revolution," Time, March 31, 2003, http://content.time.com/time/specials/packages/article/0,28804,1977881_1977883_1977922,00.html.

4   Joe Myers, "Why Scientists Think We Should Be Working 3-Day Weeks," World Economic Forum, April 16, 2016, https://www.weforum.org/agenda/2016/04/why-scientists-think-we-should-be-working-three-day-weeks/.

5   Joe Robinson, "The Secret to Increased Productivity: Taking Time Off," Entrepreneur, October 2014, www.entrepreneur.com/article/237446 (accessed from Forbes.com June 17, 2017).

6   Laura Vanderkam, "14 Time Management Strategies from Highly Productive People," Laura Vanderkam, January 22, 2016, http://laura-

vanderkam.com/2016/01/14-time-management-strategies-from-highly-pro-ductive-people/.

7   Tucker Cummings, "The Pomodoro Technique: Is it Right for You?", Lifehack accessed June 17, 2017, http://www.lifehack.org/articles/produc-tivity/the-pomodoro-technique-is-it-right-for-you.html.

8   Laura Vanderkam, "Manage Your Time," Laura Vanderkam, 2017, http://lauravanderkam.com/books/168-hours/manage-your-time/.

9   Vanderkam, "Manage Your Time."

10   Dana Malstaff, Nurture Your Business: How I Run My Business When I'm Overwhelmed and Under Water, Episode 105, podcast audio, BossMom, August 26, 2016, https://boss-mom.com/episode-105-nurture-your-busi-ness-how-i-run-my-business-when-im-overwhlemed-and-under-water-with-dana-podcast/.

11   Malstaff, "Nurture Your Business."

Chapter 13

1   Mary Kathryn Johnson, Do You Love What You Do, And Does It Make You Money?, Episode 216, podcast audio, Parent Entrepreneur Power, April 24, 2018, http://www.parententrepreneursuccess.com/do-you-love-what-you-do-and-does-it-make-you-money/.

2   Susan Krauss Whitbourne, "The Importance Of Vacations to Our Physical And Mental Health," Psychology Today, June 22, 2010, https://www.psychologytoday.com/blog/fulfillment-any-age/201006/the-impor-tance-vacations-our-physical-and-mental-health.

3   Whitbourne, "The Importance Of Vacations."

Chapter 15

1   Johnson, Do You Love What.

ACKNOWLEDGEMENTS

This book wouldn't have been possible without the working moms who shared their stories. I cannot express my gratitude for all that you shared. You peeled back the curtain to give me an intimate glimpse into your lives and shared your experience, insights, and advice. This book reflects so much of what I learned from you.

I cannot thank Robin Kegerise, Carrie Sharpe, and Danielle Tenconi enough for their time, thoughts, and insights during the early stages of this book. You each went above and beyond what I asked for, and your advice helped shape the book.

To Holly Edger, who helped me think through the initial ideas behind Mompowerment. Thank you. I'm so happy to call you a friend.

Alexa Bigwarfe, you have been a great publisher. I'm thankful for your insightful guidance and advice along this journey. To my editor, Betsy Rhame-Minor, thank you for clarifying my ideas and always answering my questions. It's been a pleasure to work with you.

My Mompowerment tribe has been such a blessing. Thank you for your continued encouragement and honesty in asking tough questions and providing insightful answers to my questions.

To my parents, I'm thankful for your continued support. I appreciate all that you do for us.

Robert, my sweet, supportive husband, I appreciate your love and enthusiasm. I am beyond thankful for the countless hours of IT help and your stellar cooking skills!

To my boys, Aiden and Evan, I love you to the moon and back more times than I can count. You keep me grounded and give me inspiration for creating more work-life balance.

ABOUT THE AUTHOR

Suzanne Brown is a strategic marketing and business consultant, work-life balance consultant and strategist, speaker, and author of *Mompowerment: Insights from Successful Professional Part-time Working Moms Who Balance Career and Family*.

She has experienced how hard it can be to juggle all the things as a working mom while in the corporate world and as an entrepreneur. Over time Suzanne realized that there were limited resources for working moms on different ways to better manage balance. She set out to provide resources to empower moms to create what they want and need on their own work-life balance journey.

Suzanne received her MBA, Bachelor of Business Administration, and Bachelor of Arts in Spanish from The University of Texas at Austin. She and her husband live in Austin, Texas. In their downtime, you can often find them trying to keep up with their two active young boys, whether on a local hike or a far-off adventure.

Read more from Suzanne about topics related to work-life balance for working moms and find more resources and templates at **www. mompowerment.com**.

Printed by Amazon Italia Logistica S.r.l.
Torrazza Piemonte (TO), Italy

16240592R00126